1001 Trump Facts
The Life, Accomplishments,
and Legacy of Our 45th
President.

By W. Jorden

Contents

Donald's Life Before Public Service.
Facts 1-39

Donald John Trump was born June 14th 1946 at the Jamaica Hospital Medical Center in Queens New York City.

After High School Trump attended the Wharton School of Finance.

Both the Phillies and Red Sox sent scouts to check up on Trump when he played first baseman in school. Trump chose not to play professional baseball because he thought he could make more money in real estate.

Trump is the fourth of five children by Frederick Christ Trump and Mary Anne MacLeod Trump, a frugal, upper middle class family with conservative values.

Trump was not allowed to own pets growing up and he is the first President in over 120 years not to have a pet in the White House. Although his first Secretary of Defense James Mattis's nickname is "Mad Dog".

In the late 1970's and early 80's Trump drove around Manhattan in a silver Cadillac with a vanity license plate that read "DJT."

Trump was raised in the Jamaica Estates neighborhood of Queens, New York City.

At age 13, he was enrolled in the New York Military Academy, a private boarding school for 5 years. As a senior, Donald Trump achieved the status of cadet captain. He was also captain of the baseball team and he played soccer as well.

Trump started college at Fordham University, but then transferred to the University of Pennsylvania Wharton School for its real estate studies program. While there he worked at the family business, Elizabeth Trump & Son. Even as a student, Trump invested in Philadelphia's real estate. Donald graduated in 1968 with a bachelor's degree in economics.

Wharton classmates of Trump, who described Trump as a vocal but unexceptional student, who rarely partook in campus activities and instead often pursued his business career.

For the December 1969 draft lottery Trump's birthday, June 14, received a high number that would have given him a low probability to be called to military service even without the 1-Y classification.

According to a Gallup poll in December 1988, Trump was the tenth most admired man in America.

One of Trump's first jobs as a young boy was to collect the change out of the washing machines from the apartments his father owned. Accompanied by his mother Trump would dash out of the car, run to the machines to get the change, then run back to be driven to the next apartment.

Trump didn't drop his football fantasies after playing varsity football in high school. In 1983, he purchased the New Jersey Generals of the United States Football League, which he unsuccessfully tried to merge with the National Football League.

Donald Trump attended Obama's White House Correspondents' Association Dinner in 2011 when Trump was considering running against Obama in the next election. The dinner turned out to be an ambush for

Trump. Obama, who commanded the microphone, made jokes at Trumps expense all night. Afterwards, Trump stayed classy and said "The President was making jokes about me. I was having a great time. I was so honored, and honestly, he delivered them well."

Although Trump's parents were considered wealthy, all of the Trump children held after-school jobs when they were young.

As a child, Donald asked to borrow his brother's blocks to build an extra tall skyscraper. After Donald finished with his construction, Donald glued the pieces together so he would never have to give them back.

In 1968 Trump was diagnosed with bone spurs in his heels, granting him a 1-Y medical deferment.

In 1988, Trump was considered as a possible running mate for George H. W. Bush, but Dan Quayle ultimately won the position.

In 1987, Trump bought what was then the world's third-largest yacht, which he named the Trump Princess, for $29 million. He never spent a night on the luxury yacht, admitting that "it makes him nervous to relax."

Early media profiles of Trump claim he graduated "first in his class" from Wharton. The evidence suggests otherwise and yet Trump has never tried to correct or clarify the error.

Bill O'Reilly asked Trump if he was a protester in the 1960s. Trump responded, "I wasn't a protester, only inwardly. I wasn't marching [in] the streets as many people were. I said, 'why are we going there?' So, I thought Vietnam was a bad war. Now at the same time, I was very young and probably shouldn't be making judgments at that age. You're supposed to rely on your great leaders. But that was a big mistake for a lot of people."

When Donald Trump studied economics at Fordham he distinguished himself from the other freshmen by always wearing a well-tailored suit. Jackets were required in the classroom but suits were rare.

Trump grew up going to Sunday school on Saturdays every weekend.

Donald's father often wore a tie in his leisure time and expected good behavior of his children. Donald was described as competitive and aggressive in a time where James Dean was redefining adolescence. It is unclear exactly what made Fred Trump send his son to Military Academy but most scholars attribute it to Donald being full of energy, more so than his parents could handle.

Donald acknowledges that his parents made the right decision in sending him to Military Academy and said that his five years there shaped his view of the world. Many of the teachers there at the time were ex-drill sergeants and combat veterans of WW2

According to Jill Brooke, a TV writer for the *Post*, Donald himself was responsible for engineering the biggest headline of his career up unto that time by calling the *Post's* editor-in-chief, Jerry Nachman, and telling him that Maples (his soon to be second wife) was gossiping to friends that Trump was responsible for "the best sex she ever had."

Attendance for Trump's second marriage in 1993 included O. J. Simpson, Rosie O'Donnel, Senator Alphonse D'Amato, and Don King.

The first time Trump ran for the President was in 2000 for the Reform party. He mentioned Oprah as his running mate but stopped running after 4 months blaming discord within the party.

Republicans wanted Trump to run for the governorship of New York in 2014 but he said he had bigger plans.

Donald registered as a Republican in Manhattan in 1987, switched to the Reform Party in 1999, the Democratic Party in 2001, and back to the Republican Party in 2009. He made donations to both the Democratic and the Republican party, party committees, and candidates until 2010 when he stopped donating to Democrats and increased his donations to Republicans considerably.

Trump was an active member of the "birther" movement that questioned President Obama's birthplace. He even sent investigators to Obama's native Hawaii to back up his accusations. When Obama publicly released his birth certificate in 2014, Trump referred to his "so-called birth certificate, or whatever it was."

Trump was voted "Ladies Man" of his class in the New York Military Academy.

In 2009, Trump filed a lawsuit against the author of the book, *TrumpNation: The Art of Being Donald*, Timothy O'Brien, for $5 million. In the book the author cited three unnamed sources who estimated Trump's net worth between $150 million and $250 million. However, the court ruled that Trump wasn't able to prove that the author committed "actual malice" and dismissed the defamation lawsuit. According to Trump's lawyers, his estimation has been "proven conclusively" to exceed $7 billion.

Donald Trump's first network interview was on the show *Rona Barrett Looks at Todays $uper Rich.*

In 2007, Trump dumped thousands of dollars from the rafters of a WWF event the "Battle of Billionaires" to upstage Vince McMahon.

Within two days following the attacks on the World Trade Center Trump arrived with over two hundred workers to help save people trapped in the rubble. 18 years later as president he signed the 9/11 victim compensation fund act.

Trump does not believe in the climate change hysteria, once stating the "Nobel committee should take the Nobel Prize back from Al Gore."

Donald Trump attended Obama's White House Correspondents' Association Dinner in 2015. He sat at a table with Martha Stewart, Billie Jean King, actress Kelly Rutherford, Brody Jenner, and Bill O'Reilly who had invited him.

The Trump Family.
Facts 40-71

Trump's older brother Freddy Trump Jr. was an alcoholic and passed away in 1981 but not before telling his younger brother Donald to stay away from alcohol. Donald confessed that the toughest situation he's ever had was in losing his older brother and because of this he has lived a sober life.

Between his three wives, Trump has 5 children.

Melania is Trump's third wife. For their wedding cake, Trump got a five-foot-tall, seven-tier Orange Grand Mariner cake. The cake weighed 200 pounds and it was covered in 3000 roses made of icing and was one of the most expensive ever made, costing at least $50,000.

Donald had his son Don Jr. get his first paying job at 14 as a dock attendant in Atlantic City before making him work in landscaping. After the change, Don Jr. complained to his dad about having to work harder and make less money, Donald responded, "Why would I pay you more than you're willing to work for?" Teaching his son a valuable lesson.

Trump's ancestors originated from the German village of Kallstadt in the Palatinate on his father's side, and from the Outer Hebrides in Scotland on his mother's side.

In 1977, Trump married the Czech model Ivana Winklmayr and they had three children. Donald Jr. Ivanka and Eric.

In 1998, Trump met a Slovenian model Melania Knauss and they married in 2005

Trump is a Presbyterian like his mother's side of the family and his ancestors on his paternal grandfather's side were Lutheran.

Frederick Trump, Donald's German grandfather came to New York City alone at 16 years old in 1885. After making money as a barber he took his savings to Seattle whose population was only 15,000 where he built restaurants and hotels. After that, he built more lodging establishments in mining towns across Oregon, Alaska, and the Yukon before finally settling down in New York City.

Donald Trump's father started E. Trump & Son with his mother because he was too young to sign contracts at the time. By the time he passed away in 1999, he had built and managed 27,000 apartments and houses in Brooklyn and Queens.

Trump said of his father, "It's because of him that I learned, from my youngest age, to respect the dignity of work and the dignity of working people. He was a guy most comfortable in the company of bricklayers, carpenters, and electricians—and I have a lot of that in me also."

Trump believes that "If you don't drink and you don't do drugs, your children are going to have a tremendously enhanced chance of really being successful and having a good life."

George A Sorial who worked with Trump for almost a decade said that Trump was often tougher on his kids who worked for him than the rest of his employees.

As a testament to his father raising him when Don Jr. talks about the Trump Organization he says, "We're the world's largest mom-and-pop company."

Don Jr. describes his dad as "just a blue-collar guy with a large bank book."

Trump's wife, Melania, is the second foreign-born First Lady of the United States, following Louisa Adams in 1825.

When his kids were growing up, as teens and preteens, Trump had them work on job sites and learn about stonemasonry, plastering, plumbing, and carpentry. Even 12-year-old Eric learned to cut rebar with an acetylene torch to help construction workers when renovating Seven Springs. Trump made sure his kids learned these and other skills that would enable them to have an understanding of trades required when entering real-estate development.

When Eric Trump was only 6 years old Donald would send him off to school telling him "Remember, no drinking, no drugs, and no smoking and get good grades."

When Eric Trump was asked about what his father would like to be known for when he passes away Eric said, "He would want to be known as a great builder, a person who changed skylines and amassed some amazing iconic projects around the world, before anything else. He'd be proud of being president, of course, and fighting for what's right for the country, at great personal cost. But, to this day he is proudest of the things he has built and is always keen to build more. He can't help himself. That's his true and ultimate passion."

The Trump family never went on vacations and his kids learned to love work. Even Hillary Clinton praised Trump for teaching his kids to love ambition.

In September of 1998, Trump attended a New York Fashion Week party at Manhattan's Kit Kat Club, near Times Square when he first saw Melania Knauss. He stated, "I went crazy. I was actually supposed to meet somebody else. There was this great supermodel sitting next to Melania. I was supposed to meet this supermodel. They said: 'Look, there's so and so.' I said: 'Forget about her. Who is the one on the left?' And it was Melania."

Melania said of her first meeting with Trump, "He wanted my number, but he was with a date, so of course I didn't give it to him. I said, 'I am not giving you my number; you give me yours, and I will call you.' I wanted to see what kind of number he would give me — if it was a business number, what is this? I'm not doing business with you." Trump in return gave her every number he had so she could reach him no matter where he was.

Trump's grandchildren are Jewish.

Despite people saying that Trump is a racist and hates immigrants he has dated a black woman and married two immigrants.

Trump was in the room for the birth of his 4th child and even cut the umbilical cord himself.

Donald Jr. remembered growing up with his father, "If we wanted to see him, we could see him. If we called, he could be in the middle of the most important meeting, he'd take the phone call. If we wanted to show up in his office, we could play trucks while he's dealing with the biggest guys in the banking finance. We'd be making noise, and he was totally fine with it. He wasn't, 'Let's go in the backyard for two hours and play catch.' That wasn't his thing. He had some of what Fred had: 'Come spend the day with me and we can go to the job site. You can watch me deal with things. You can watch me do deals in the office.' But it wasn't a traditional [upbringing].

Trump named his youngest son Barron after the legendary hotel mogul Barron Hilton.

Fourteen years after joining the family business and becoming President of the company Donald Trump amassed a billion dollars in assets for the Trump Organization.

Trump's first wife was Ivana Zelnickova, a Czech national who had immigrated to Canada to escape communism. The two met at a singles bar on the Upper East Side of Manhattan and were married the next year.

The dinner tables when Donald was growing up didn't include much talk of politics, religion, or current events but business was a constant topic.

It's never been clearly defined how Trump met his second wife, Marla Maples. Tabloids from the time suggested it was a chance encounter on Madison Avenue but few people close to Trump believe that.

Don Jr. said of his dad's parenting, "He's not a teacher that puts you on his lap and says this is how you do something. He puts you in a situation to learn, and you rise to the occasion or you fail."

The Man, The Myth, The Legend.
Facts 72-142

Trump's favorite books include *The Bible*, *All Quiet On The Western Front*, and Sun Tzu's *Art of War*.

Don Jr. has gone on record to say that his dad has never admitted to making a mistake. He added, "I think he recognizes that in the world of mob mentality, you get no credit for being sorry. You get no forgiveness; you get no quarter."

Trump amassed so many movie and television credits because in all of the filming contracts if you use one of Trump's buildings as a filming location he must be given a cameo.

Trump's show *The Apprentice* has two Emmy nominations.

Trump once offered Obama the chance to play golf for free at any of his golf courses. He offered this with the strict stipulation that Obama resigns his presidency.

Trump made 5.6 million dollars a year as the host on *The Apprentice*. That equals $375,000 per episode.

Trump eats like many Americans. He loves fast food but his favorite food is steak. Trump has often made fun of and looked down upon by well to do individuals for putting catchup on his steak but many Americans who aren't well off and therefore can't afford nice steaks choose to put ketchup on their steaks.

Like Ronald Regan, Trump has a star on the Hollywood walk of fame. They are the only two presidents with stars.

Often when Trump's hair gets too long his wife Melania cuts it.

Trump took part in the ALS Ice Bucket Challenge with Miss Universe and Miss USA doing the honors of pouring the ice water on him

Spy magazine sent Trump at check for 13 cents just to see if he would cash it. He did.

Trump is a member of the Screen Actors Guild.

Trump is half Scottish, loves Scotland and owns many properties there.

Trump is six foot three inches making him the third tallest president behind Abraham Lincoln (6'4") and Lyndon B. Johnson (6'3.5"). George Washington who was known for his towering height comes in fourth place at six foot two inches.

Trump's twitter gains an average of 67,000 followers every month.

Trump first denounced David Duke, a clan member over 20 years ago.

Trump Tower was used as Wayne Enterprises in the Batman film *The Dark Knight Rises*.

Trump's favorite movies are *Citizen Kane* and *Gone With The Wind* but he's also mentioned he loves Jean-Claude Van Dame's action film *Bloodsport*.

Donald Trump rarely drinks coffee or eats a big breakfast.

Trump works 85 hours a week and sleeps 4 hours a night.

He did this as a businessman and now reportedly as President.

Trump offered to be Mike Tyson's personal financial advisor.

As a child, Trump attended the First Presbyterian Church in Jamaica, Queens. This is also where he had his confirmation.

He has stated that he has never smoked cigarettes or used drugs, including marijuana.

Trump has called golfing his primary form of exercise.

Trump headlined *WrestleMania* 23 in 2007 and a *Monday Night Raw* in 2009.

Trump has made cameo appearances in 12 films and 14 television series, including one for his role in *Home Alone: Lost in New York* and one as the father of one of the characters in *The Little Rascals* (1994).

Trump opposes legalizing recreational marijuana but supports legalizing medical marijuana.

Trump goes to church on Sunday as often as he can and always on Christmas, Easter, and other major occasions.

Trump has never tried to fight off the label of "billionaire playboy."

In 2007, Trump entered into a bet with WWE Chairman Vince McMahon. The two men each chose a pro-wrestling representative to fight on their behalf and the billionaire whose fighter lost the fight had to shave his head. When it was all said and done Trump helped shave McMahon's head.

Mark Burnet who developed the show *The Apprentice* said of Donald's personal character, "Donald will say whatever Donald wants to say. He takes no prisoners. If you're Donald's friend, he'll defend you all day long. If you're not, he's going to kill you. And that's very American. It's like the guys who built the West."

The 58-story Trump Tower is 664 feet (202 m) high, making it the 64th tallest building in New York City. The top story is marked as "68" because, according to Trump, the five-story-tall public atrium occupied the height of 10 ordinary stories.

Trump owns the painting *Two Sisters* (On the Terrace) an 1881 work by French Impressionist artist Pierre-Auguste Renoir, which he keeps in his penthouse.

Donald Trump has up to 15 bottles of Diet Coke a day and always with ice in a glass. There's a red button in the Oval Office and whenever he pushes it someone brings him his Diet Coke.

Trump turned the 5th floor of the Trump Tower into a fully functional television studio so that he could work in his penthouse then take the elevator down for when it was time to film.

Trump believes that homosexual couples have the same adoption rights as straight couples.

Bill O'Reilly describes Donald Trump as a "no" person. As in "no doubt, no fear, no apologies, no retreat", and "no quarter for his enemies."

Donald Trump's name is in the title of at least 15 studio

songs from artists such as Young Jeezy and Mac Miller.

One of Donald Trump's favorite Presidents is Andrew Jackson, the 7th President of the United States who participated in several duels.

George A Sorial who has known Trump for over a decade and worked with him closely has only ever seen Trump in blue jeans one time. Trump either wears a suit and tie or his golf attire.

Trump thinks the word "tweet" is juvenile and prefers to refer to them as his messages on social media.

Wax figure artists from Madame Tussauds visited Trump in 1997 to measure him for a life-size wax replica of him for their museum. According to their measurements, Trump's hand measures 7.25 inches from the tip of his middle finger to his wrist.

Trump said in a UN Speech in 2017, "The problem in Venezuela is not that socialism has been poorly implemented, but that socialism has been faithfully implemented."

Trump's office in the Trump Tower is on the 26th floor and he has a private elevator.

Trump thinks that the government should classify Bitcoin as a legal currency.

Trump believes citizens should not be allowed to save or invest their money in offshore bank accounts as too many wealthy citizens are abusing loopholes in offshore banking laws to evade taxes.

Trump feels that the government should prevent "mega

mergers" of corporations that could potentially control a large percentage of market share within its industry.

Trump believes there should be more restrictions on current welfare benefits.

Trump said he would require businesses to be required to provide paid leave for full-time employees during the birth of a child or sick family member.

It's been proven that women have been paid to accuse Trump of crimes he didn't commit.

Trump thinks that the government should regulate the prices of life-saving drugs.

Trump thinks that the military should allow women to serve as long as they can pass the same physical tests as men.

Trump has been in Burger King, Pizza Hut, Diet Pepsi, and Oreo commercials.

Trump says that after a psychological examination to show they fully understand this choice, terminally ill patients be allowed to end their lives via assisted suicide.

Trump chose not to support removing references to God on money, federal buildings, and national monuments.

Trump believes that marital rape be classified and punished as severely as non-marital rape.

Trump doesn't think that universities should provide "trigger warnings" and "safe spaces" for students.

Trump says that a business should be able to deny

service to a customer if the request conflicts with the owner's religious beliefs.

Trump often receives Bibles from fans in the mail, when he receives them he either stores them or gives them away to others.

Trump said of his use of Twitter and the hundreds of thousands of people who read his tweets, "It's like owning a newspaper without the losses."

When Trump is in a new town he likes to get the local paper to get to know the concerns of the locals.

Trump has internet news articles printed for him to read.

Trump does not diet or exercise much because he believes it would change the look of his face, which he does not want.

Trump has attended multiple same-sex marriage ceremonies.

Here's what Bill O'Reilly, who has gotten to know Trump well, had to say about Trump's feelings on Muslims, "Donald Trump is not sympathetic to that religion's culture. He is deeply offended that the Muslim world has not risen up en masse against jihad. As a New Yorker, he took 9/11 very personally and does not believe it benefits that nation to accept many Muslim immigrants. It's not about ethnicity for Mr. Trump; it's about the soft reaction to terrorism in the Islamic world."

Trump fought alongside locals to stop a wind farm from going up in Scotland because it would hurt the value of his golf course and the local's homes.

Trump tweets around 370 times a month.

Mocking the environmentalist movement supported by the left to switch to paper straws Trump began selling plastic MAGA straws and they sold out completely. Trump's straws are recyclable whereas the paper straws aren't recyclable. Inadvertently creating something better for the environment.

At first, The Washington post attacked Trump for putting a $50,000 golf simulator in the White House. When all the facts arrived it turned out that Obama had installed it at taxpayers' expense and that Trump had it upgraded out of his own pocket. Despite the truth, The Washington Post never issued a retraction.

When Trump misspelled press "coverage" as press "covfefe" in a tweet journalist argued over what the hidden meaning meant.

Trump in Business.
Facts 143-193

Trump wine comes from a vineyard and winery that Trump owns in Charlottesville, Virginia.

Between 1990 and 2009 Trump filed for bankruptcy for six of his businesses. Also, Trump has over 500 businesses that haven't gone bankrupt.

By the time he was 27, Trump owned 14,000 apartments throughout Staten Island, Queens, and Brooklyn.

Through his negotiating skills, Trump reportedly was able to convince the city of New York to give him a 40-year tax break which saved him over a million dollars over that period.

Trump is a published author. His first book *The Art Of The Deal* was on the *New York Times* Best Seller list for 48 weeks and was number one for 13 of those weeks. As of 2016, over 1.1 million copies have been sold.

Only one-third of Trump's business ventures become successes with another third found some success but only lasted a few years and the final third never got off the ground. This makes his success rate better than the national average. For instance, only one in ten silicon valley businesses makes any profit.

Trump owned Miss Universe, Miss USA, and Miss Teen USA beauty pageants.

Trump released a board game through Milton Bradley in 1989 called *Trump: The Game*.

Trump says that board members of a business should be

the most qualified regardless of gender.

Trump owns 18 golf courses around the world.

Trump took charge of his family's real estate business in 1971 and renamed it The Trump Organization. He also expanded it from Queens and Brooklyn into Manhattan.

In 1988, Trump acquired the Plaza Hotel in Manhattan for $407 million.

Donald Trump began construction on Trump Tower when he was only 33 years old.

Trump's businesses have hosted several boxing matches at the Trump Plaza in Atlantic City, including Mike Tyson's1988 heavyweight championship fight against Michael Spinks.

In 1989 and 1990, Trump lent his name to the Tour de Trump cycling stage race, which was an attempt to create an American equivalent of European races such as the Tour de France or the Giro d'Italia.

In 1988 and 1989, Trump hosted Wrestle Mania IV and V at the Trump Plaza in Atlantic City.

At one point, Trump casinos reportedly employed more than 8,000 people and accounted for nearly one-third of Atlantic City's gambling revenues.

The Apprentice ran for 11 years with Trump, which is a long time for any show to run.

When Trump became company president, his father the chairman said "Donald has a competitive spirit, and I don't want to compete with him."

Trump said, "the finest piece of real estate in the world is at the corner of 5th Avenue and 57th street." That's where the Tiffany building was located until Trump bought it and built the Trump Tower.

When Trump published his first book, *The Art of the Deal*, he also started The Donald J. Trump Foundation to donate a portion of profits from book sales to charities.

Trump bought new paintings to be put up in Turnberry, his golf course in South Ayrshire, Scotland and was insistent that he and his son Eric put them up as he was too excited to wait for others to do it for them. For two hours Donald and Eric walked around the hotel hanging paintings as a crowd grew, not believing that a global celebrity would be personally involved in what seemed to be a trivial task. This very thing happened on more than one occasion.

When Trump is working in Trump Tower he eats in the cafeteria downstairs rather than going out to a fancy restaurant.

When Trump was approached with the idea of the TV show *The Apprentice* he said that reality television "was for the bottom-feeders of society".

According to the US Patent and Trademark Office website, Trump tried to file a trademark application for the phrase "I'm back and you're fired!"

Bruce Willis, Johnny Carson, and Steven Spielberg have all lived in apartments inside the Trump Tower. And through a Panamanian holding company so did the deposed and despised dictator of Haiti, Jean-Claude Duvalier, who secretly purchased an apartment.

Trump has written several books of business advice, including T*rump: How to Get Rich* and *Why We Want You to Be Rich*: *Two Men--One Message.* According to Random House, Donald Trump is the greatest selling business author of all time.

When Trump bought a golf course under construction that would become the new Trump National Golf Club Bedminster he helped iron out the details. One particular issue was what to do with the 60 or so people who had already paid tens of thousands of dollars to be original members under the last business administration. Trump didn't have to honor their memberships but he did and he also made them honored founding members. Initially this cost him millions of dollars but he knew they'd appreciate the gesture and pay their annual dues for a long time.

During Christmas Holiday parties at the Trump World Tower, Trump would have all the employee's names written on pieces of paper and draw them out of a hat. Winners could get as much as $15,000 from having their name drawn.

Playing golf to Trump is not about relaxation, it's simply a new setting to conduct business. While he plays Trump routinely takes phone calls, meetings, and makes complex business decisions.

Even before he became President, Trump nicknamed his private Boeing 757 jet Trump Force One. The plane is configured to seat 43 and is fitted with a dining room, bathroom, shower, bedroom, guest room, and galley. Many fixtures are plated in 24k gold.

Trump banned Jeffrey Epstein (known pedophile, sex trafficker, and a self-claimed initial funder of The Clinton

Foundation) for life from his Mar-a-Lago club when he learned about the rumors of Epstein's sexual conduct.

Trump hates overpaying for anything, especially real estate which was rising exponentially in the 2000s. Because of this he stopped buying properties and began to diversify the company in the time just before the 2008 housing market crash. A move that possibly saved the company. Moreover, once the crash happened the Trump Organization had cash on hand to buy property for literally ten cents on the dollar.

When Trump wants to add someone to his team in the Trump Organization and that person is currently working for someone else, Trump makes a personal call to their employer for permission to make an offer. If the employer says no for whatever reason Trump won't make an offer to hire the person.

Trump once hired the director at a military museum to be the executive vice president of Trump International Golf Links Scotland. When Sarah Malone told Trump she knew nothing about Golf he responded "That's even better. I don't want someone on this project wasting their time playing golf!"

Trump would not require employers to be required to pay men and women the same salary for the same job as there are too many other variables such as education, experience, and tenure that determine a fair salary.

Trump has never had a computer on his work dest.

When Trump became president he was no longer legally allowed to run the Trump Organization so he created trusts and named his children and longtime CFO Allen Weisselberg as trustees.

Sarah Malone said that Trump is a perfectionist and one day when Trump was visiting his Scottish course he noticed a piece of window sill had been chipped off. He continued to bring up the window sill all day asking if it had been fixed yet but the maintenance department was busy and hadn't gotten to it yet. At the end of the day, Trump had someone bring him the necessary wood filler and paint to fix it himself, which he did in his business suit.

In a private conversation with Alex Salmond, a Scottish politician who was working against Trump's prized golf course in Scotland, Trump told him directly "Alex, if you fight with me, be warned, I hit below the belt."

Donald Trump was able to avoid having to be bossed around by New York City's organized crime, which even controlled some of the labor unions in the city, by staying close to the political figures of NYC. Figures such as mayor Abe Beame who attended Trump's first wedding and Governor Hugh Carey who Trump donated generously to.

In the late '70s, New York City was riddled with crime and was close to bankruptcy. Because of this real-estate was cheap and the perfect opportunity to begin buying property in Manhattan. Donald Trump first purchased the dilapidated Commodore Hotel which is close to Times Square and Grand Central Station. Donald teamed up with the Hyatt Hotel company and turned the Commodore into the popular Grand Hyatt Hotel making Donald a power player in New York.

Trump has never filed for personal bankruptcy but a few of his businesses have at a rate of about one out of every 83 businesses he owns.

The Wollman Skating Rink in Central Park fell into disrepair and the city's Parks Department said it would take two years to get back up and running. After six years and $13 million spent the rink was no closer to opening until Trump came along. Trump promised he'd have it done in six months for no more than $3 million. Salvaging noting Trump started from scratch and finished the rink in four months and at a final cost 25% below budget.

When Donald Trump gave the job of constructing Trump Tower to Barbara Res he was appointing the first woman ever to lead a skyscraper project.

According to Donald Trump Jr., there was some contention between his father and Grandfather when the two started working together. Fred seemed to be happy being a millionaire and didn't need to be a billionaire but Trump did and was willing to take more risks.

At one point the Trump Organization had 50% equity in the Empire State Building. Trump fought to rename it the "Trump Empire State Building Tower Apartments."

Many years before becoming President, Trump was asked by Robert Mueller if he could get his $15,000 deposit back from his club membership at a Trump golf club. Trump refused because it violated company policy.

Trump never had a problem being bullied around New York City once he began his real estate career like others did because Roy Cohn was his personal lawyer. Roy was chief counsel during the McCarthy hearings in 1954.

When Trump became President, his family, who were now in charge of the Trump Organization stopped doing international business deals so that to minimize any conflicts of interest.

Sarah Malone who headed Trumps Scotland golf course said "Trump is a very progressive employer. He's not interested in gender; he's just interested in results."

Awards And Honors.
Facts 194-221

Trump received the Tree of Life Award by the Jewish National Fund in 1983.

Trump received the Ellis Island Medal of Honor in celebration of "patriotism, tolerance, brotherhood and diversity" in 1986. He received this award alongside Rosa Parks and Muhammad Ali who also received the same award.

In 1995 Trump received the President's Medal by the Freedom Foundation for his support of youth programs.

Trump was entered into the Gaming Hall of Fame in 1995 for his contributions to the gaming and entertainment industry.

Trump received a Humanitarian Award by the National Jewish Health in 1976.

Trump received the Muhammad Ali Entrepreneur Award in 2007.

Trump received the Unicorn Children's Foundation Shining Star Award in 2008.

Trump has received multiple AAA Five Diamond Awards for this hotels.

Trump received the Palm Tree Award by the Palm Beach Police Foundation in 2010.

Trump received the Presidential Hero Award by the Lois Pope LIFE Foundation in 2011.

Trump received the Presidential Order of Excellence from Georgia in 2012

Trump was inducted into the WWE Hall of Fame in 2013 during Wrestle Mania 29.

Trump was inducted into the New Jersey Boxing Hall of Fame in 2015.

Donald Trump was featured on the cover of Playboy magazine in March of 1990. 26 years later he brought an original copy of the magazine to one of his rallies in Pennsylvania.

Trump received The Algemeiner Liberty Award for his contributions to Israel-United States relations in 2015.

Trump received the Marine Corps-Law Enforcement Foundation Commandant's Leadership Award in 2015.

Trump received the first-ever Lifetime Achievement Stevie Award at The 3rd Annual American Business Awards in 2006.

Donald Trump was *Time Magazine*'s Person of the Year in 2016.

Trump received the Friends of Zion Award by The Friends of Zion Museum in 2017.

Trump was Sports Business Journal's Most Influential Person in Sports Business in 2017

To honor Trump for recognizing Jerusalem as Israel's capital the Mikdash Educational Center released a Temple Coin featuring his likeness.

Beitar Trump Jerusalem renamed themselves by adding Trump's name to honor him for recognizing Jerusalem as the countries capital in 2018.

Trump was inducted into the Atlantic City Boxing Hall of Fame in 2018.

Trump received the 2018 Wounded Warrior Project Award to commemorate his support for the group during the 2018 Soldier Ride.

Trump was named one of Time Magazine's 100 Most Influential People in the World in 2019.

Trump received the Medal of Bravery from the Afgan people by Logar Province in 2018.

In 2010 Trump was awarded an honorary degree in business administration from the university but then revoked the degree once he became President because of comments Trump made on Muslims entering America.

Trump received a Bipartisan Award for Criminal Justice reform in October 2019.

Trump's Good Deeds.
Facts 222-251

In 1995, a motorist stopped to help Trump after the limo he was traveling in got a flat tire. Trump asked the good samaritan how he could repay him for his help. The man only asked for a bouquet of flowers for his wife. A few weeks later Trump sent the flowers to their home with a note that read: "We've paid off your mortgage."

In 2008, after Jennifer Hudson's family members were tragically murdered in Chicago, Trump put her and her family up at his Windy City hotel for free. In addition to that, Trump's security took extra measures to ensure Hudson and her family members were safe during such a difficult time.

Trump bought Mar A Lago, a segregated private estate and when he reopened it as a private club Jews and blacks were finally allowed to join. The town fought Trump on this but he sent every member of the town council copies of movies about discrimination: *Guess Who's Coming to Dinner* and A *Gentleman's Agreement*. Trump finally won out in a pubic court of opinion.

Trump launched a crowd-funding site which ensured that a young Mexican-American boy with a terminally-ill mother could attend college.

In 1988 when a sick 3-year-old Orthodox Jewish, Andrew Ten, needed a flight from California to New York for special treatment Trump dispatched his private jet when no airline would accommodate the boy's elaborate life-support system.

In 2013 when Trump heard bus driver Darnell Barton saved a woman from jumping off a bridge he sent him

$10,000. Trump said, "Although I know to you it was just a warm-hearted first response to a dangerous situation your quick thinking resulted in a life being saved, and for that, you should be rewarded."

In 1986, Trump prevented the foreclosure of Annabell Hill's family farm after her husband committed suicide. Trump personally phoned down to the auction to stop the sale of her home and offered the widow money. Trump decided to take action after he saw Hill's pleas for help in news reports.

In 1991, 200 Marines who served in Operation Desert Storm spent time at Camp Lejeune in North Carolina before they were scheduled to return home to their families. However, the Marines were told that a mistake had been made and an aircraft would not be able to take them home on their scheduled departure date. When Trump got wind of this, he sent his plane to make two trips from North Carolina to Miami to return the Gulf War Marines to their loved ones.

In 1996, Trump filed a lawsuit against the city of Palm Beach, Florida accusing the town of discriminating against his Mar-a-Lago resort club because it allowed Jews and blacks. Abraham Foxman, who was the Anti-Defamation League Director at the time, said Trump "put the light on Palm Beach – not on the beauty and the glitter, but on its seamier side of discrimination." Foxman also noted that Trump's charge had a trickle-down effect because other clubs followed his lead and began admitting Jews and blacks.

In 2000, Maury Povich featured a little girl named Megan who struggled with Brittle Bone Disease on his show and Trump happened to be watching. Trump said the little girl's story and positive attitude touched his heart. So he contacted Maury and gifted the little girl and her family with a "very generous check."

In 2014, Trump gave $25,000 to Sgt. Andrew Tahmooressi after he spent seven months in a Mexican jail for accidentally crossing the US-Mexico border. Obama never tried to get Andrew back to the US.

In 2016, Melissa Consin Young attended a Trump rally and tearfully thanked Trump for changing her life. She said she proudly stood on stage with Trump as Miss Wisconsin USA in 2005. However, years later she found herself struggling with an incurable illness and during her darkest days she explained that she received a handwritten letter from Trump telling her she's the "bravest woman, I know." She said the opportunities that she got from Trump and his organizations ultimately provided her Mexican-American son with a full-ride to college.

Lynne Patton, a black female executive for the Trump Organization, released a statement in 2016 defending her boss against accusations that he's a racist and a bigot. She tearfully revealed how she's struggled with substance abuse and addiction for years. Instead of kicking her to the curb, she said the Trump Organization and his entire family loyally stood by her through "immensely difficult times."

Trump loaned his personal jet to Nelson Mandela.

Al Sharpton and Jesse Jackson personally thanked Donald Trump for his private donations to several African American scholarship funds.

Trump was on the board of directors of several charitable organizations, including the Police Athletic League and the United Cerebral Palsy.

Trump upgraded MLK's birthplace to a national historic park when he became president.

As President, Trump posthumously pardoned legendary boxer Jack Johnson.

Trump established an Opportunity & Revitalization Council to restore insalubrious black neighborhoods.

Trump granted Alice Johnson clemency.

March 9, 2018. The White House announced that President Trump had pardoned Kristian Saucier, a Navy sailor who unlawfully took pictures of a classified room in a submarine and whose crime was compared to that of Hillary Clinton who was not punished for herself mishandling classified information.

April 13, 2018. President Trump pardoned Scooter Libby, an aide to former Vice President Dick Cheney who had been convicted in 2007 for obstruction of justice after a special counsel investigation criticized by conservatives. Though many conservatives advocated for pardoning Libby before Trump's action, former President George W. Bush only chose to commute his sentence.

August 25, 2017. Trump's first pardon was granted to former Arizona sheriff Joe Arpaio, who was convicted of criminal contempt for disregarding a court order in a racial-profiling case.

May 24, 2018. President Trump posthumously pardoned Jack Johnson, the first boxing champion who was black, something previous administrations such as the Bush and Obama administrations refused to do.

May 31, 2018. President Trump pardoned conservative activist Dinesh D'Souza, who had been convicted in 2014 for making an illegal campaign contribution.

July 10, 2018. President Trump pardoned Dwight and Steven Hammond, two ranchers who were given unusually long sentences for setting a controlled fire that spread to federal lands, something which had inspired protests from conservative ranchers including Ammon Bundy.

May 6, 2019. President Trump pardoned Army Lieutenant Michael Behenna, who had been convicted in 2009 of killing a suspected Iraqi terrorist prisoner and who had broad support for a pardon.

Trump used to own the Miss Universe and Miss USA pageants. Controversy arose when Miss USA 2006 Tara Conner was caught breaking pageant rules by drinking and other activities. Trump gave her a second chance after personally speaking with her and allowed her to retain her crown as she attended rehabilitation. For several weeks after this, Rosie O'Donnell berated Trump for his decision on The View.

Each quarter since taking office, President Trump has donated his salary, fulfilling a promise he made to the American people.

In 2019 Trump signed H.R. 2423 to honor Women's Suffrage with the Centennial Commemorative Coin Act. The bill directs the Treasury Department to create currency that honors the women who played a major part in the passage of the 19th Amendment, which was ratified in 1920.

Running For President.
Facts 252-309

When Trump first told Bill O'Reilly that he was thinking of running for president they were at a Knicks game and Bill responded comically, "Of what country?"

On June 16th, 2015 Trump announced his intention to run for president at Trump Tower in New York.

During the 2016 election, 62% of all Google searches for GOP candidates were for Trump. Jeb Bush was second with 9%.

According to the William Hill Betting Agency in 2015 Trumps odds of winning the 2016 election were 100 to one.

Trump said his wealth would make him immune to pressure from campaign donors.

Trump was one of seventeen candidates vying for the 2016 Republican nomination; this was the largest presidential field in American history at that time.

It is estimated that 1.4 million Americans attended a Trump campaign rally in 2016.

Hillary Clinton said in 2013, "I would like to see people like Donald Trump run for office. They're honest and can't be bought.

Trump won the Republican primary, receiving more votes than any other Republican primary candidate in history.

On the campaign trail in 2016, Alva Johnson tried to sue Trump for grabbing her hand and pulling her into him to kiss her on the lips without her consent. Two years later video surfaced of the incident where you can see Trump never grabbed her hand and the "kiss" was actually a common European style greeting. Both Trump and Alva lean in and turn their faces in opposite directions and kissed off to the side of the other person. His lips never touched her and the conversation that she said happened afterward is shown in the video to have never happened.

Respected polls such as the Princeton Election Consortium put Trump's chances of victory at 1 percent on election night. In the last 24 hours of the campaign, the New York Times, tracking various posters' models, concluded that Trump's chances of winning in such surveys were 15%, 8%, 2%, and less than 1%. When a progressive poll master Nate Silver suggested before the vote that Trump had a 29% chance of winning the Electoral College democrats grew angry at him for suggesting such a high percent.

Eight out of every ten white evangelicals voted for Trump.

Nineteen Women have accused Trump of sexual assault. Seventeen of those women did so only after Trump announced he was running for President and the majority of them in the month before the 2016 election. Of the two women who accused him before that time one was his first wife during their divorce. Not a single one of these women have ever filed a police report.

In 2016, Forbes ranked Trump as the 336th wealthiest person in the world and 156th in the United States, at a net worth of $4.5 Billion.

Donald Trump made 323 campaign appearances compared to Hillary Clintons 278 events.

The Apprentice's season one finale garnered 28.1 million views which equates to 17.76% of the registered number of voters in the 2016 election.

Trump chose Mike Pence, the governor of Indiana as his running mate because of his low-key, Christian profile in hopes of balancing out Trump's flamboyance and to help attract the Evangelical vote that rejected Mitt Romney in 2012.

Trump, in a 1990 Playboy magazine interview Trump said "We Americans are laughed at around the world for losing a hundred and fifty billion dollars a year, for defending wealthy nations for nothing... Our allies are screwing us." He echoed the same thing when he ran for president 26 years later.

CNN made so much money from Trump's debates that he requested they donate some of the money to Veterans.

By the time Trump's last primary opponent had dropped out of the Republican race Trump had the support of only 40% of Republicans. But on election day 88% of Republicans voted for him.

Trump was very happy to announce during his run for the presidency "For the 1st time in American history, America's 16,500 border patrol agents have issued a presidential primary endorsement—me!"

Trump said, "Becoming the nominee of the party of Abraham Lincoln has been the greatest honor of my life."

During the transition period, the Obama Administration engaged in surveillance and information-gathering of Trump, to investigate any alleged ties to Russia. This was confirmed by GOP U.S. Representative Devin Nunes on

March 22, 2017, and by Evelyn Farkas, the deputy assistant secretary of defense under Obama, on March 29, 2017.

In the first Presidential debate, Trump said he'd release his tax returns once Hillary released her 33,000 deleted emails.

Despite expectations that Trump's election victory would cause the markets to plunge, the Dow Jones Industrial Average performed very strongly, closing at the highest level it had ever reached in history after the second day. It's rare for the stock market to rise immediately after a U.S. presidential election regardless of the winner. The stock market had its best week in five years due to optimism of a Trump presidency.

With the historic flip of Elliott County, Kentucky, every rural, white-majority Southern county voted for the Republican nominee for the first time in history.

Trump won more votes in the general election than any Republican candidate in U.S. history.

96% of campaign contributions from the media didn't go to Trump but went instead to Clinton.

According to a study, 91% of the media coverage concerning Trump was negative when he was running for president.

Trump had pledged, if elected president, to appoint a special prosecutor to further investigate Hillary Clinton's use of a private email server whilst Secretary of State, but Hillary took her defeat so hard that Trump softened his stance after winning.

Donald Trump spent $93 million on TV ads as opposed to Hillary's $253 million. However, Trump did far more free television appearances than Hillary.

Governor Mike Huckabee, a candidate for the Republican nomination dropped out and said of how Trump defeated all the candidates, "Donald's strategy of dominating media coverage worked. Republican voters wanted to blow up the system, and Trump promised that. The rest of us could not get to know because the press was not interested in us. It was all about Donald and whatever attacks he was launching."

At the first Republican debate Trump had the most talking time at ten minutes, thirty-two seconds and Jeb Bush, who was considered the front runner, was second with eight minutes, thirty seconds.

Trump was strongly endorsed by the National Rifle Association in one of its earliest endorsements in an election campaign.

As president, Trump has promised to re-arm military personnel on all American military bases as well as ROTC recruitment centers, which were disarmed by the Clinton Administration.

In February 2011, Trump announced that he is pro-life, and at the final presidential debate on Oct. 19, 2016, Trump gave the strongest endorsement of the pro-life position of any presidential nominee in history.

President Donald Trump believes that millions of people voted illegally in the US election. He first made the claim in a tweet in late November 2016. A recent analysis of voting data agrees that Hillary Clinton may have received at least 800,000 votes from illegal aliens.

From the day Trump declared he was running for president to the day he won was only 551 days.

At the end of Trump and Hillary's second debate, they were asked to say something good about the other person. Hillary complimented the Trump children and Trump said Hillary was persistent: "she doesn't give up."

Liz Crokin is an entertainment journalist and covered Trump for a decade before he ran for office. She admits she can get paid "a lot of money" to dig up dirt on celebrities like Trump but she never heard anything negative about him until he started running for President.

The Super Tuesday turnout was massive in 2016. The Republicans had 8.5 million votes compared to 4.7 in 2012 when Mitt Romney was the Republican headliner.

Russia donated zero dollars to the Trump campaign but has donated $145,600,000 to the Clinton Foundation.

About 82 million American's watched Trump and Hillary's first debate and 66 million watched the second.

Similarly to Reagan's slogan "Let's Make America Great," Trump himself chose to use "Make America Great Again."

When Trump was interviewed by Playboy magazine in 1990 about what political party he'd run as if he ever ran for president he responded, "Well, if I ever ran for office, I'd do better as a Democrat than as a Republican, and that's not because I'd be more liberal, because I'm conservative. But the working guy would elect me. He likes me. When I walk down the street, those cabbies start yelling out their windows." Studies of the 2016 election show that most working-class people did vote for Trump, has he predicted, even though he ran as a Republican.

During Trump's first debate with Hillary the moderator, Lester Holt, interrupted Trump 41 times and only interrupted Hillary 7 times. This is also the debate where Hillary was given the questions days in advance by CNN's Donna Brazile.

Donald Trump's first interview after announcing his bid for the 2016 presidential campaign was with Bill O'Reilly on The O'Reilly Factor. Bill's first question was about how Trump would defeat ISIS who which Trump talked about finding the best Generals to get the job done. When Bill pressed for specific details Trump responded, "I'm not telling you anything. And the reason I'm not is because I don't want [ISIS] to know the game plan."

Don Jr. was watching his father when the news outlets were declaring him the victor and said "My father does not show emotion. The magnitude of this had not yet hit him. Everyone around him was saying, 'I can't believe we won.' But he said very little. He just continued to watch the coverage."

Twenty-four million people watched the first Republican debate, the largest cable news audience in history with much of the credit given to Trump. Possibly the biggest sound bite of the night came when Megyn Kelly accused Trump of having referred to women as "fat pigs, dogs, slobs, and disgusting animals" to which Donald Trump comically responded, "Only Rosie O'Donnell."

Trump said that the reason he detested FOX News host Megyn Kelly so much during the 2016 race was that he felt she grilled him much harder than the other candidates and that she was using him to get famous.

Donald Trump refused to be on the debate stage for the 7th Republican debate in 2016 because Megyn Kelly was to be a moderator. As a result that debate had half the TV audience attendance.

In an interview with Bill O'Reilly, Trump was asked if anything Hillary said during their first debate stuck out in his mind. Trump responded, "I think there is...I saw when she's talking and talking about what she's going to do and how she's going to do it—I realized she's been doing this for 26 years to 30 years, and nothing ever gets done. Even when she went to the United States Senate from New York, she said she was gonna bring back jobs to New York, and it was a disaster. Upstate New York is a total disaster. And I started to say, "Wait a minute, Hillary, you've been there 26 years, and you haven't done it. Why all of a sudden are you gonna do it? You're not going to do it."

Two days before Trump and Hillary's second debate and only a month before the election video surfaced from 2005 of Trump having a lewd conversation about women. Trump issued the following statement, "I've never said I'm a perfect person, nor pretended to be someone that I'm not. I've said and done things I regret, and the words released today on the is more-than-a-decade-old video is one of them. Anyone who knows me knows these words don't reflect who I am. I said it, I was wrong, and I apologize... We'll discuss this more in the coming days. See you at the debate." Trump also described the recorded conversation during the debate as "locker room talk" and reminded everyone about Hillary's husband's behavior.

Before Trump and Hillary's second debate Trump held a press conference and the three women he invited to speak were Paula Jones, Kathleen Willey, and Juanita

Broaddrick who have all accused Bill Clinton of sexual misconduct. They were then joined by Kathy Shelton, a rape victim at 12 years old whose assailant was represented by Hillary when she was a public defender. Trump was trying to show his supporters that there's a stark contrast between his "words" and the actual misdeeds of the Clintons.

On election day 2016 the Clinton Campaign rented the Javits Center for it's anticipated victory party. The land under the center was sold to New York City by Donald Trump.

Whereas Hillary had rented a stadium the day of the election with many big-name celebrities chosen to speak, Trump rented an intimate ballroom at the New York Hilton Midtown Hotel with no big speakers; although there was an ambitious man selling pretzels out front but he had left by 7 pm.

In 2016 Trump won Michigan by a 0.2% margin, Pennsylvania by 0.7%, and Wisconsin by 0.8% all of which were swing stages and none had been won by a Republican for 20–30 years.

Before Trump walked out onto the stage to give his victory speech the night of winning the 2016 Presidential election he turned to a dear friend who congratulated him and said "We still have a long road to come, George. There's a long haul ahead."

Inauguration Day.
Facts 310-325

The night before Trump's inauguration he and his family stayed at the Blair House, across the street from the White House as per tradition.

Trump's first tweet the day of inauguration was at 7:15 a.m. and read "It all begins today! I will see you at 11 a.m. for the swearing-in. THE MOVEMENT CONTINUES— THE WORK BEGINS!"

Don Jr. said this about election day with his father, "It was business as usual. We always expect success and never talk about failure. My father thought they might pull something. Even though we were all beaten down [from campaigning,] we were still at war. Nobody relaxed. We were like caged animals."

Just before the inauguration, Trump met with Obama for more than an hour and supposedly got along well. Obama confided that North Korea would be Trump's biggest problem and that hiring General Michael Flynn as a national security adviser would be a mistake. After this, they rode in the same limousine to take them to the swearing-in ceremony.

Don Jr. greeted his father when he arrived for the inauguration, he noted "He never shows emotion, but he was in awe of what was happening. He said to me, 'Now we'll find out who our friends are.' He wasn't nervous about his speech because he's a game-time player, but he was focused on it. He planned to stick it to the establishment. He was also concerned about the size of the crowd because we were hearing the Park police were keeping people away."

Donald Trump's inauguration speech was only fifteen minutes long. According to one reporter citing anonymous sources George W. Bush had the strongest reaction to his speech saying, "That's some weird shit."

At Trump's inauguration at least 217 protesters were arrested.

Upon his inauguration, Trump delegated the management of his real estate business to his two adult sons, Eric and Don Jr.

President Trump's inauguration did have a smaller in-person turnout than Obama's first Inaugural address. Also, Obama had 8 million more people watching on television than Trump although it is estimated that if online viewings were totaled Trump would have had more people watching.

On his first day in the White House with his grandchildren racing through the many halls and rooms, Trump turns to his oldest son and says, "I wish my mother and father were alive to see this."

On the same day as his inauguration, Trump filed for re-election in 2020, breaking the political norm, giving him a head start on campaigning, and giving him additional legal freedoms and flexibility.

His first bill signed as president was to allow retired general and Defense Secretary nominee James "Mad Dog" Mattis to be confirmed.

Trump returned the bust of UK Prime Minister Winston Churchill to the Oval Office that Obama removed when he took office. He also accepted the United Kingdom's offer to re-loan the second identical bust of Churchill, which

Obama removed and returned after the first loan expired.

Trump instituted this day as a national day of patriotism and a few days later Trump officially designated his inauguration day the National Day of Patriotic Devotion.

On his first day in office Trump ordered a regulatory freeze on all federal governmental agencies.

Trump instituted a federal hiring freeze from which the military was exempted. Then in April the administration partially lifted the hiring freeze and replaced it with a plan to restructure the executive branch and decided against filing numerous governmental positions. This was all aimed at shrinking the executive branch of the government.

The 45th President.
Facts 326-405

Donald J. Trump is the 45th President of the United States.

Trump's most popular tweet to retweet came the day after he was elected president. It read "TODAY WE MAKE AMERICA GREAT AGAIN!" It has over 526,000 likes and has been retweeted over 229,000 times.

At 70, Trump is the oldest first-term elected President beating Ronald Reagan who was elected at 69 years old.

Trump is the only President who has never drank alcohol, keeping a promise he made to his older brother who was an alcoholic.

Donald Trump is the 5th president in U.S. history to lose the popular vote but gain the office.

Dr. Martin Luther King Jr.'s niece, Dr. Alveda King says she never endorses Presidential candidates, however; she said publicly she was glad he won and has often been photographed with him.

January 23, 2017. Three days after taking office Trump signed an order that withdrew the United States from the "globalist" Trans-Pacific Partnership, which was negotiated by Obama incentivized outsourcing. Long opposed by FAIR, a key feature of the trade agreement was a "temporary entry" guest worker program that would have increased immigration without a say from Congress (which has plenary authority over immigration) or the American people.

January 24, 2017. Trump signed an order requiring the United States Secretary of Commerce make a plan within six months mandating all new or improved pipelines be made with American steel, another order requiring every federal agency to streamline manufacturing regulations, and the third allowing fast-track approval for important infrastructure projects.

January 25, 2017. Trump signed an executive order that included ordering the "immediate construction of a physical wall on the southern border," the hiring of 5,000 additional border control agents, and ending "catch-and-release" policies for illegal immigrants.

January 25, 2017. Trump signed an executive order that called for hiring an additional 10,000 federal immigration officers, re-establishing the Secure Communities Program and other local partnerships, making the deportation of criminal illegal immigrants a priority, directing the State Department to use leverage to ensure countries-of-origin take back illegal immigrants and stripping federal grant money from sanctuary cities and states. It was reported in early August 2017 that due to reforms and additional hirings of immigration judges, the number of deportation orders increased by nearly 28%.

January 27, 2017. Seven days after taking office President Trump signed a memorandum to begin the expansion and rebuilding of the U.S. military.

In Trump's first 100 days in office, the U.S. national debt decreased by $100 billion, as opposed to Obama's first 100 days where the debt grew by $560 billion. While the national debt passed the $20 trillion mark during the fiscal year 2017, the rate of growth was less than half the average during the Obama Administration. Also, the Trump Administration made moves to reduce the need to borrow money.

Trump is the first president without prior military or government service.

Trump chose his daughter Ivanka to be the personal assistant to the president.

In December 2015, Harold Bornstein, who had been Trump's personal physician since 1980, released a letter stating that Trump "will be the healthiest individual ever elected to the presidency".

Trump is the first billionaire American president.

January 31, 2017. President Donald Trump announced he would keep a 2014 executive order signed by former President Obama that gave protected status to homosexual employees of the government and federal contractors.

It was reported on June 10, 2017, that President Trump had signed 37 bills into law, more than each of the previous four presidents at the same point in their presidencies, and the U.S. House had passed 158 bills, "making it the most productive in the modern era," according to GOP House leaders.

During the three years since Trump announced his presidential run in 2015, Forbes estimated his net worth declined 31%.

Whenever there's a dog on Air Force 1, President Trump makes it wear booties.

Trump marked the official start of the reelection campaign with a rally in Melbourne, Florida, on February 18, 2017, less than a month after taking office.

On May 22, 2017, Trump was the first U.S. president to visit the Western Wall in Jerusalem and when he arrived he kissed it.

In mid-July 2018, Trump was pronounced by experts in Washington to have suffered the worst ten days of his presidency. During this time was the Russian summit and the subsequent sloppy press conference with Russian President Putin in Helsinki, Finland. Also during this time his now-indicted former lawyer Michael Cohen made news coverage. CNN then released an example of attorney Cohen's secretly recorded old conversations with Trump about possible payments to a long-ago paramour. And if that weren't enough media predictions about the course of Robert Mueller's investigation filled the remaining time of news coverage. Despite all of this negativity in the media, an NBC/WSJ poll showed that Trump's favorability climbed and with near-record approval from Republicans.

Trump in 2019 gave official U.S. recognition to the Golan Heights as being part of Israel and for recognition for his support of Israel, a plaza in Jerusalem was named the Donald Trump Square. In addition, Israeli Prime Minister Benjamin Netanyahu unveiled a sign at the proposed site of a Golan Heights settlement to be named Trump Heights.

After his election as U.S. president, Israeli Prime Minister Benjamin Netanyahu called Trump "a true friend of the State of Israel."

Like President Ronald Reagan, Trump never removes his suit jacket while in the West Wing of the White House.

May 2, 2019. For the first time in its history, the U.S. sent a delegation to the March of the Living, an annual Jewish

Holocaust commemoration in Poland.

By mid 2019 Trump has sold a million MAGA hats. 62,984,828 people voted for him in the first election so he has sold almost one MAGA hat for every 63 people who voted for him.

The Washington Post reported that 91 percent of Trump's news coverage was negative during the summer of 2017. This was based on research by the Media Research Center who came to a similar conclusion for early 2018.

Donald Trump was the first President that supported gay marriage coming into office. Obama didn't come out in support of gay marriage until he had already been sworn in.

Trump was the first President to mention support for gays in a presidential acceptance speech when he said, "I will do everything in my power to protect our LGBTQ citizens."

Trump was the first President to launch a global campaign to decriminalize homosexuality in the world.

According to the Media Research Center at the end of 2017 and beginning of 2018, there were only 12 minutes of news coverage of the growth of the economy and jobs, 9 minutes of positive coverage for Trump's tax cuts, and coverage of military successes against al Qaeda and ISIS received only eighty-three seconds.

Analyzing ABC, CBS, NBC, evening newscasts in January and February of 2018 devoted 63% of news about Trump to scandals.

Trump usually eats dinner at the White House and rarely goes out to socialize, unlike the Obamas who would eat out. He uses this time to be with his wife and youngest son Barron.

A 2017 Quinnipiac University poll showed that 80% of Republicans trust Trump more than the Media.

A YouGov poll commissioned by the London-based periodical The Economist found that at least 70% of Republicans trust Trump more than the *New York Times*, the *Washington Post*, and *CNN*. *Fox News* faired a little better with 54%.

As President, Trump has played a round of golf with Tiger Woods.

Trump didn't stop campaigning after he won the nomination in 2016 and has continued holding rallies. He's the first President to ever go on a nationwide victory tour and every rally since 2016 has sold out.

In March of 2018, the conservative Heritage Foundation had concluded that the Trump administration, in a little over a year of governance, had already implemented two-thirds of its 334 agenda items. Compare that to Ronald Reagan who had only finalized about 49%.

A November 2017 Quinnipiac poll showed that 58% of Americans objected to the way the media covers Trump and only 38% approved.

The Associated Press found in late 2018 that late-night hosts made more jokes about Trump than any other public figure in history.

Former president Jimmy Carter who was criticized heavily during his presidency stated that the media was more biased against Trump than any other president he knew about.

At the beginning of the third year of his first term as president, Trump has seven female top advisers, as compared to five for Obama, three for Bush, and five for Clinton at that point in their presidencies.

In the first six weeks of Trump's presidency, over 90 regulations were repealed, whether through executive orders, Acts of Congress, or other means aimed at promoting a smaller government and helping business.

Trump said that the U.S. government should not bail out Puerto Rico.

Trump thinks the Federal Reserve Bank should be audited by Congress.

Trump said that labor unions, in theory, help the economy but have recently become corrupt and should have their powers limited.

In Trump's first three years in office, his staff can only remember him watching one movie, *Midnight Express*, the 1978 story of a young American imprisoned in Turkey on drug charges.

Trump said he would not add "Gender Identity" to anti-discrimination laws.

Trump was the first sitting American president to address the annual Values Voters Conference in Washington.

In August of 2019 Trump's assistant, Madeleine Westerhout was discovered to have been leaking information to the media. A week before this news story broke the hot topic in the media was about Trump supposedly saying the U.S should try to nuke a hurricane to stop it. During this time Michael Knowles of The DailyWire wrote an article about how he thinks Trump said this crazy thing about nuking a hurricane to a private group to intentionally see if it was leaked to the press in an attempt to discover a leaker. Because of stories like this, there is a growing number of people that believe Trump is playing 4D chess.

At the G-20 summit in Germany, President Trump wore an American flag pin, being the only world leader not to wear the G20 pin which had globalist symbolism.

August 22, 2017. President Trump's own words of what his political movements stood for: "This evening, joined together with friends, we reaffirm our shared customs, traditions, and values. We love our country. We celebrate our troops. We embrace our freedom. We respect our flag. We are proud of our history. We cherish our Constitution, including, by the way, the Second Amendment. We fully protect religious liberty. We believe in law and order. And we support the incredible men and women of law enforcement. And we pledge our allegiance to one nation under God."

October 17, 2017. Speaking at a Heritage Foundation event, President Trump stated that "the most important truth our Founders understood was this: Freedom is not a gift from government; freedom is a gift from God." He also stated that "young Americans should be taught to love our country, honor our anthem, and proudly recite the pledge of allegiance."

December 8, 2017. At a rally in Pensacola, Florida, President Trump stated, among other strongly-conservative statements that "America is a sovereign country. We set our immigration rules. We do not listen to foreign bureaucrats. We do not listen to other countries telling us how we should be running our immigration." He also stated that "we proudly pledge allegiance to one nation, under God. Our rights come from our creator, and no earthly force can ever take those rights away, and they never will. That is why my administration is taking power back from global bureaucrats and returning that power back to the American people... We don't sing a global anthem. Our troops don't wear a foreign uniform. And we will never surrender our rights to international tribunals. We won't do that. We proudly sing The Star-Spangled Banner. Our brave troops fight and die in red, white, and blue, and we protect and preserve the American Constitution that we cherish. I've said it so often, my job is not to be president of the World. My job is to be President of the United States of America."

June 5, 2018. After disinviting the Philadelphia Eagles to a White House event because many of the team's players decided to boycott it, President Trump held a "Celebration of America" that honored the United States and its military.

October 22, 2018. President Trump held a large rally in Texas for Senator Ted Cruz, where he made strongly conservative statements, including accusing Democrats of launching "an assault on the sovereignty of our country." He also strongly rejected globalism and labeled himself a nationalist, something he defended the next day. The rally helped Cruz beat Beto and get reelected.

January 17, 2019. After Speaker of the House Nancy Pelosi disinvited President Trump to give his State of the Union Address because of a partial government shutdown, Trump denied the use of military aircraft for Pelosi for the same reason 30 minutes before she was set to begin a trip outside the country.

March 2, 2019. President Trump spoke at CPAC for the third consecutive time in his presidency, giving a strongly conservative two-hour speech. Among other statements, he criticized the Mueller investigation, mocked the Green New Deal, defended campus free speech, defended his tariff-friendly trade policy, and spoke in favor of the Second Amendment.

President Trump donated his entire first-quarter 2017 salary to restore the Antietam National Battlefield.

Trump's presidential campaign advocated against Nanny State policies such as banning plastic straws.

Trump explored the option of purchasing Greenland, which is subsidized by Denmark. Greenland's Foreign Minister Ane Lone Bagger said that "We are open for business, but we're not for sale" and declined. The U.S. already has a military base in Greenland but the purchase would provide the U.S. with its abundant natural resources like iron ore, zinc, and oil. It turns out China is trying to get a foothold in Greenland and right next to a U.S ballistic missile defense system there.

Trump enjoys giving tours of the White House and knows vast amounts of history about the different rooms and objects within them.

Three years into Trump's first term he hasn't turned in his tax returns and neither has Nancy Pelosi who is third in line for the Presidency.

Trump has confided that his youngest son, who is only 13, worries about how much the media hates his father. When asked how he responds Trump answered, "I always say: we just keep going forward, that's what we do. you know, the media doesn't care if they hurt families. They are the meanest people. But when I leave office, I'll have my revenge. Because many of them will go out of business. Without Trump, what have they got?"

Democrats are currently trying to impeach Donald Trump just like they have tried to impeach every Republican President since Eisenhower.

President Trump filed a lawsuit to block a New York subpoena of his tax returns in 2019.

Trump has been known to attend the weddings of ordinary people who voted for him and randomly sent him an invitation.

A 2019 study by sociologists at the University of Pennsylvania found that the U.S. had become less racist under President Trump.

Trump invited victims of illegal aliens to the State of the Union whereas Nancy Pelosi invited illegal aliens.

According to a Real Clear Politics average of more than a half dozen major polls Trump's approval rating in September 2019 was higher than Obama's at the same point in his presidency. Even with 92% negative media coverage Trump's approval rating is 44.3% whereas Obama's was 43.9% with mostly favorable coverage.

Michael Cohen was Trump's personal lawyer for about ten years, he told the world Trump was a racist and a crook. Either he truly believes this or he was upset at the president and wanted vengeance for not pardoning him for his crimes of income tax evasion among other things.

CNN ran a story about how Trump wanted to nuke hurricanes because they're African.

When Nancy Pelosi announced impeachment proceedings on Trump it fired up his base and they took action by donating. Trump received $15 million in donations in just a few days and the National Republican Congressional Committee's online fundraising went up 608 percent.

Donald Trump turned down Robert Mueller when he wanted to head the FBI after James Comey was fired.

When Trump was asked how the media's hatred has affected him he responded, "In one way it's positive. It shows that I can take it. Not many people could get through what I've had to take. Rudy Giuliani's a tough guy but he told me he doesn't think he could handle all the hate."

The Mueller investigation lasted two years and cost the taxpayers 32 million dollars. Robbert Mueller's staff included 40 FBI agents, intelligence analysts, forensic accountants, and other personal staff. The investigation issued 2,800 subpoenas, 500 search warrants, obtained 230 orders for communication records, issued almost 50 orders authorizing the use of pen registers, made 13 requests to foreign governments for evidence, and interviewed about 500 witnesses. In the end, the Mueller investigation did not find evidence that the Trump campaign "coordinated or conspired with the Russian government in its election-interference activities".

Trump said the hardest thing he's had to do as president is sign the letters to the families of fallen soldiers.

Trump moved several agency divisions out of Washington, D.C., and into the areas of the U.S. that they were created to serve. For example, the Agriculture

Department moved two of its research agencies to Kansas City. Additionally, the Interior Department announced it would move the Bureau of Land Management's headquarters to Colorado.

Rolling Back Red Tape And Cutting Costs.
Facts 406-443

President Trump has followed through on and exceeded his promise to roll back at least two regulations for every new one created. In 2017, the Trump Administration eliminated 22 regulations for every new one. The Administration's focused on reducing regulations for of "furthering individual liberty and property rights" along with economic reasons. Among those economic reasons, it was reported in June 2017 that President Trump's deregulation actions had increased confidence and hiring in the manufacturing sector.

President Trump's Administration surpassed the 2:1 ratio in 2018 by eliminating 12 regulations for every new one.

According to the Competitive Enterprise Institute, the Trump Administration issued the fewest number of new regulations in its first two years compared to any other administration since the regulatory state's establishment.

According to a May 2018 report by the American Action Forum, the Trump Administration was on track to double the amount saved and the number of regulations cut compared to its goals.

According to the Competitive Enterprise Institute in October 2017, Trump was the "least regulatory president" since Ronald Reagan and was even faster than Reagan in advancing his conservative deregulation agenda.

March 31, 2017. President Trump signed another bill undoing an Obama-era regulation, giving the power back to the states to expand drug testing for unemployment benefit applicants. Much of the regulation Trump rolled back were those created by Obama.

April 3, 2017. President Trump signed a bill reversing an Obama-era FCC privacy regulation applicable to internet service providers. The FCC had adopted the rule to fill a gap created by a court case that ruled that the FTC did not have jurisdiction to extend its privacy rule over internet service providers because they were regulated by the FCC. The new law repealed the FCC rule and prohibits the FCC from enacting a replacement for 10 years without giving the FTC jurisdiction to regulate internet service providers' privacy practices. Part of yet another series of bills undoing other Obama regulations.

May 12, 2017. President Trump signed Public Law 115–33 (S. 496), which repealed a rule by the Department of Transportation that would have taken power away from local governments on infrastructure planning.

Trump used the Congressional Review Act to repeal regulations more times than any other President in history. Before Trump's presidency, the Congressional Review Act had been used only once successfully, sixteen years prior. When the window to use the CRA for Obama-era regulations ended, Congress had passed and Trump had signed 14 CRA resolutions repealing Obama regulations. These actions were estimated to have saved $3.7 billion in regulatory costs and up to $36.2 billion in compliance costs.

In the first 11 months of Trump's presidency, his administration imposed $5.8 billion in new regulations, as opposed to $24.8 billion in the last 16 days of Obama's presidency.

By July 2017. The Trump Administration had withdrawn or effectively killed 860 proposed Obama era regulations, including 179 that were on a secret list of proposed regulations.

In addition to cutting regulations, President Trump had a successful first year in reducing the number of federal government employees. By early August 2017, the Trump Administration had reportedly reduced the number of federal employees by 9,000 even with an increase in Pentagon employees. By the end of September 2017, every cabinet department – with the sole exceptions of the departments of Homeland Security, Veterans Affairs, and the Interior – had fewer permanent staff than they had at the beginning of the year. Overall, the number of federal employees fell by 16,000 during this time, and it was the first time since Bill Clinton's presidency that the number of federal employees fell during a president's first year in office.

May 16, 2019. The Trump Administration formally canceled a $929 million grant to California for the state's high-speed rail program.

In 2017, the Trump Administration saved $774 million by beginning to privatize FEMA flood insurance risk.

February 24, 2017. President Trump signed an executive order requiring every federal agency to create a "regulatory reform task force" to find unnecessary, burdensome regulations to repeal. This order was called "the most far-reaching effort to pare back U.S. red tape in recent decades." By August 2018, twelve of 22 federal agencies had met or exceeded the regulatory savings target set by President Trump in 2017.

April 25, 2017. President Trump signed an executive order ordering the Department of Agriculture to find and eliminate unnecessary regulations, in a direct effort to help farmers, particularly in the light of NAFTA and the trade imbalance with Canada.

Trump signed legislation to roll back costly and harmful provisions of Dodd-Frank, providing relief to credit unions, and community and regional banks.

April 26, 2017. President Trump signed an executive order ordering the Interior Department to review designations of national monuments from as far back as 20 years prior, with the intention of reversing federal overreach in land acquisition and returning power to the states.

April 21, 2017. President Trump signed one executive order directing the Treasury Secretary Mnuchin to look at the U.S. tax code and recommend the removal of unnecessary regulations.

February 28, 2017. President Trump announced that he did not plan on filling numerous government positions he considered unnecessary. According to one source, about 2,000 positions were vacant, and most of them were likely included in this list. As of April 4, 2017, President Trump did not make a nomination for nearly 500 positions requiring Senate confirmation.

March 28, 2018. President Trump signed a bill into law that created a permanent ban on the use of federal funds for official portraits, though it only cut a small amount of federal waste.

February 27, 2018. The White House announced President Trump had reached an informal deal with Boeing that would save the U.S. government $1.4 billion – with the new price at $3.9 billion – for two new Air Force One planes. Similarly, the Defense Department suspended F-35 Lighting II deliveries due to a dispute with Lockheed over who should pay for a production mistake in the jets.

April 12, 2018. President Trump signed an order creating a task force to review the finances of the United States Postal Service.

May 24, 2018. President Trump signed a directive ordering federal agencies to reduce regulations for private space travel companies.

As the White House's staff was significantly smaller than under the Obama Administration – 374 people in 2018 versus 469 in 2010 – the Trump Administration White House was able to cut its payroll by over $5 million compared to the Obama Administration's 2015 payroll and had saved a total of $11 million by 2018.

Since taking office, President Trump's deregulation efforts have achieved $33 billion in regulatory savings. In 2018, these efforts alone delivered $23 billion in benefits to American families and business owners. Federal agencies achieved more than $8 billion in lifetime net regulatory cost savings from rolling back regulation.

August 30, 2018. Because of budgetary problems caused by overspending, President Trump canceled a planned across-the-board 2.1% pay raise for civilian federal employees, saving the government about $25 billion.

October 17, 2018. President Trump asked each of his cabinet members to cut spending in their departments by at least 5%.

June 20, 2018. The U.S. Senate rejected a Trump administration plan to cancel $15 billion in spending. The Trump Administration originally wanted to cut spending by $60 billion, but Mitch McConnell rejected this, forcing the Administration to propose a more modest cut.

April 24, 2019. President Trump signed an executive order transferring responsibility for background checks of federal employees from the Office of Personnel Management to the Defense Department.

June 11, 2019. President Trump signed an executive order directing federal agencies to simplify regulations for genetically modified food.

June 14, 2019. President Trump signed an executive order directing federal agencies to reduce their advisory committees by at least one-third.

March 13, 2017. President Trump signed an executive order to perform an audit on every executive branch agency to reduce spending and waste and improve services.

President Trump signed an executive order to streamline the permitting process for infrastructure projects with a goal of cutting approval time from up to 10 years to an average of 2 years.

September 4, 2019. The Trump Administration announced it would repeal Bush- and Obama-era regulations on lightbulbs.

October 9, 2019. President Trump signed two executive orders to rein in the administrative state, limiting the use of agency guidance, increasing White House oversight over agency guidance, and requiring them to go through the same process as regular regulations.

October 10, 2019. President Trump signed an executive order requiring federal agencies to offset administrative spending increases with spending cuts elsewhere.

October 31, 2019. President Trump signed an executive order repealing a 2009 order signed by Obama that had placed limits on the hiring options of federal contractors.

Economy, Tax Cuts, And The American Worker.
Facts 444-497

Due to President Trump's pro-growth policies, real gross domestic product (GDP) growth exceeded 3 percent over the last four quarters of 2018. Real GDP grew at annual rates of 3.4 percent in the third quarter of 2018 and 4.2 percent in the second quarter. In Trump's first year as president, the U.S. economy grew 3% even though all of the news outlets said he'd bring on a terrible rescission as soon as he took office.

In the first two years of Trump being in office over 5.3 million new jobs were created and the unemployment rate remains below 4 percent. Prior to 2019, the unemployment rate had fallen below 4 percent only five times since 1970. By the end of 2019 7 million jobs had been created.

When Trump ran for office he did so saying he'd build the economy and that resonated with his supporters. Now that the economy is booming only 12 percent of Americans rate the economy as the most significant problem facing our country, the lowest level on record.

Trump said when he first announced he was running for president "I all be the greatest jobs president that God ever created." Under President Trump, job openings outnumber the unemployed for the first time on record, and new unemployment claims recently hit a 49-year low. For the first time on record the number of job openings exceeded the number of unemployed people looking for work in March of 2018 and every month for at least the next year.

Trump as put so many people to work that since the election that 6.2 million individuals have been lifted off of food stamps.

March 27, 2017. President Trump signed an executive order repealing Obama-era labor law compliance requirements for federal contractors, along with signing a resolution of disapproval that day on the same topic.

June 15, 2017. President Trump signed executive orders to loosen federal regulations on job-training programs and to encourage apprenticeships and vocational learning.

September 29, 2017. President Trump disbanded the federal labor-management council, which was created by President Obama, due to it being a waste of time and taxpayer dollars.

November 1, 2017. President Trump signed a Congressional Review bill into law repealing a regulation enacted by the Consumer Financial Protection Bureau banning mandatory arbitration clauses in contracts regarding financial services which would allow consumers to join class-action lawsuits against banks and credit card companies.

April 10, 2018. President Trump signed an executive order calling for a government-wide review of welfare programs to ensure that they help Americans find work and escape poverty. The order also called on the federal government to create or strengthen work requirements for its welfare programs.

In addition to creating initiatives to reduce food stamp

usage, the Trump Administration cracked down on food stamp fraud. Because of this in fiscal year 2017, the federal government spent the lowest amount of money on the food stamp program in seven years. Not only that but according to the USDA, in 2017, participation in the Women, Infant, and Children (WIC) food stamp and welfare program reached its lowest level in 17 years.

President Trump is delivering on his promise to bring back American manufacturing. A poll found that 85 percent of blue-collar workers believe their lives are headed "in the right direction." Between July 2017 and July 2018, blue-collar jobs grew at the fastest rate since 1984, and they also grew faster than service jobs along the more liberal coastlines. And the Bureau of Labor Statistics also reported that blue-collar wages grew faster than white-collar wages in 2018.

Every sitting President is offered an invitation to attend the National FFA Convention. The National FFA Organization is an American youth organization to promote and support agricultural education. President Trump is the first President in 27 years to accept the invitation.

Trump's economy has broken so many records that the New York Times admitted it "ran out of words" to describe how well the economy has been doing.

Trump signed Executive Order 13788, titled "Buy American and Hire American," directed government departments to review guest worker programs and implement changes that favor American workers over cheap foreign labor. The executive order also sought to reform how H-1B visas are awarded, calling on federal agencies to suggest changes to the programs to ensure jobs go to the most-skilled or highest-paid applicants.

President Trump signed the Tax Cuts and Jobs Act into law, ushering in the largest package of tax cuts and reforms in American history. After the tax cuts, over $450 billion has poured back into the U.S., including more than $300 billion in the first quarter of 2018.

As a result of Trump's tax bill, small businesses will have the lowest top marginal tax rate in more than 80 years.

Nine in ten American workers are expected to see an increase in their paychecks thanks to Trump's tax cuts, according to the Treasury Department. And Ernst & Young found 89 percent of companies planned to increase worker compensation thanks to the tax cuts.

Trump's tax cuts are delivering results for American families and workers. In the first year more than 6 million workers received tax cut bonuses and benefits, more than 100 utility companies have announced lower rates. More than $5.5 trillion in gross tax cuts have been provided, nearly 60% of which will go to families.

Trump's tax cuts increased the exemption for the death tax to help save Family Farms & Small Businesses. Nearly doubled the standard deduction for individuals and families. It also doubled the child tax credit to help lessen the financial burden of raising a family.

Trump lowered America's corporate tax rate from the highest in the developed world to allow American businesses to compete and win. Small businesses can now deduct 20% of their business income. He also cut dozens of special interest tax breaks and closed loopholes for the wealthy.

President Trump signed an executive order establishing the National Council for the American worker.

Over 100 utility companies have lowered electric, gas, or water rates thanks to the Tax Cuts and Jobs Act.

May 24, 2018. President Trump signed a bill into law repealing some financial regulations put into place under the Dodd-Frank law, including reducing the amount of regulation and oversight for banks having under $250 billion in assets. The Act was described as the largest change to U.S. banking regulations since the Dodd-Frank law.

August 31, 2018. President Trump signed an executive order to make it easier for small businesses to offer retirement plans to their employees. The Labor Department released the finalized rule on July 29, 2019.

October 24, 2018. The National Labor Relations Board issued a memo making it easier for workers to sue their unions for negligence.

September 3, 2018. President Trump issued a strongly-worded Labor Day proclamation, praising American workers and highlighting his pro-worker policies, including on trade, deregulation, taxes, and immigration. The proclamation also stated that "in all economic decisions, we believe in our sovereign obligation to defend and protect our country's workforce, and to seek its economic interests above that of any other country." In 2018, 284,000 manufacturing jobs were created, making it the best year for manufacturing since 1997. Among other positive statistics, job security increased for factory workers compared to previous periods of economic growth.

More than 185 companies and associations have signed Trump's "Pledge to America's Workers," promising more than 6.4 million new training and career opportunities.

Trump signed legislation that reauthorized the Carl D. Perkins Career and Technical Education Act, making more than $1 billion available for career education programs. He also signed the first Perkins CTE reauthorization since 2006, authorizing another $1 billion for states each year to fund vocational and career education programs.

The Trump administration helped launch the Women Entrepreneurs Finance Initiative, which could leverage more than $1 billion to support women entrepreneurs.

Trump established opportunity zones to spur investment in left-behind communities.

Trump signed an executive order expanding apprenticeship opportunities for students and workers.

Trump's proposed infrastructure plan would utilize $200 billion in Federal funds to spur at least $1.5 trillion in infrastructure investment across the country.

Trump signed an executive order expediting environmental reviews and approvals for high priority infrastructure projects.

Under Trump federal agencies have signed the One Federal Decision Memorandum of Understanding streamlining the federal permitting process for infrastructure projects.

Trump created a rural prosperity task force and signed an executive order to help expand broadband access in rural areas.

Trump was very busy in his first week of office and showed he was serious about his campaign promises. This caused the stock market to increase, and the Dow Jones passed 20,000 points for the first time in its history. This has become known as part of the "Trump Effect".

March 27, 2017. President Trump signed an executive order repealing the contracting rule.

The number of Americans using food stamps continues declining, something attributed to new work requirements and other restrictions on food stamp use, and something which resulted in reduced dependence on the government. In April 2019, the number of individuals on food stamps fell to the lowest level in ten years, and the following month, the number of households fell to the lowest level in nine years.

May 25, 2018. President Trump signed three executive orders reforming federal workforce rules, such as making it easier to fire federal employees for misconduct, weakening the power of federal labor unions, and making the workforce more efficient and less costly. Among these changes, federal workers were required to use at least 75% of their work time to actually do the jobs they were hired to do rather than doing union-related work.

Under Trump manufacturing jobs growing at the fastest rate in more than three decades.

The stock market had one of the best performances in the first 100 days of Trump's presidency compared to the first 100 days of previous presidents in U.S. history.

June 25, 2019. President Trump signed an executive order creating the White House Council on Eliminating Barriers to Affordable Housing Development, intended to reduce regulations that made housing more expensive.

Trump's policies have created more than 400,000 manufacturing jobs since his election.

Under Trump, the median household income has hit the highest level ever recorded.

The Trump Administration continued promoting apprenticeships in 2019 as in the previous two years.

January 31, 2019. The National Mediation Board proposed a new rule that would make it easier for railroad and airline employees to decertify their labor unions.

Under President Trump, African-American poverty rates reached record lows of 21.2 percent in 2017 and African-American unemployment hit a record low of 5.9 percent in May 2018.

Under President Trump, Hispanic-American poverty rates

reached record lows of 18.3 percent, in 2017 and Hispanic unemployment fell to 4.5 percent.

Under President Trump, Asian-American unemployment at a record low of 2 percent.

Under President Trump, female unemployment dropped to 3.6 percent, which is the lowest rate in 65 years.

Under President Trump, youth unemployment recently reached its lowest level in more than 50 years at 9.2%.

Under President Trump, Americans without a high school diploma reached the lowest unemployment rate ever recorded.

Under President Trump, veteran's unemployment rate fell to 3% in 2018 and the unemployment rate for post-9/11 veterans fell to the lowest level on record.

Unleashing American Energy.
Facts 498-533

Trump promised to promote fossil fuels when he was running for President and now, two and a half years later, the U.S. is the world's largest oil producer. In addition, natural gas exports more than doubled in the first half of 2018 and in the third quarter of 2018 U.S. coal exports to countries like Honduras rose 242 percent.

Because of Trump rolling back costly and burdensome regulations U.S. oil exports in the first half of 2018 had risen 80% compared to the same period in 2017.

December 6, 2018. Directed by the President, the Interior Department announced it would roll back an Obama-era regulation protecting the sage-grouse, giving states more flexibility and opening up new lands for oil drilling while still protecting the species. The Interior Department finalized the regulation on March 15, 2019. Because of things like this the EIA confirmed that U.S. oil production comprised 98% of all global oil production growth.

February 14, 2017. Trump signed H.J.Res.41 into law, which blocked an Obama Administration regulation that would have required oil, natural gas, and mining companies to disclose any payments made to foreign governments. In 2018 the EIA reported, that oil production had hit 11 million barrels per day for the first time ever. Then the U.S. continued increasing its global energy dominance. In mid-February 2019, U.S. oil output reached 12 million barrels per day, an achievement reached well ahead of schedule, and crude oil exports reached a record high of 3.6 million.

Many of Trump's campaign positions included pursuing energy independence. As a U.S. Crude oil production has increased by 25.6%. By early 2018, the U.S. was experiencing an oil boom, having a positive effect on the nation, while at the same time reducing its oil imports.

U.S. exports increased so significantly that oil disruptions in the Middle East benefited U.S. producers. U.S. oil also flooded European markets to the disadvantage of OPEC countries and Russia, and shale oil companies earned enough money to finance new wells themselves for the first time. In December 2018, the EIA reported that U.S. oil exports increased to 3.2 million barrels per day, a new record.

March 28, 2017. President Trump signed an executive order repealing several Obama-era environmental regulations unfavorable to coal, including a January 2016 moratorium on new coal leases on federal lands.

Trump signed an action to expedite the identification and extraction of critical minerals that are vital to the nation's security and economic prosperity.

Trump took action to reform National Ambient Air Quality Standards which benefited American manufacturers.

Trump signed a Presidential Memorandum declaring that the Dakota Access Pipeline serves the national interest and initiating the process to complete construction.

Trump issued permits for the New Burgos Pipeline that will cross the U.S.-Mexico border.

The Trump Administration has streamlined Liquefied Natural Gas terminal permitting. In 2017, the United States became a net natural gas exporter for the first time in 60 years.

By May 2019, the EU increased its imports of U.S. natural gas by 272% since 2016 because of pressure from President Trump.

July 31, 2017. The United States and Ukraine agreed to have the U.S. export coal to Ukraine, so the latter could gain energy independence from Russia.

The President has ended the war on coal and increased U.S coal exports by 60 percent. He did this by cutting Obama-era regulations such as the "Stream Protection Rule" which was estimated to cost industries $81 million a year.

President Trump is replacing the Clean Power Plan, a flawed Obama-era regulation that the Supreme Court ordered halted and proposed the Affordable Clean Energy Rule as a replacement.

President Trump rescinded Obama's hydraulic fracturing rule, which was expected to cost the oil and gas industry $32 million per year.

Trump proposed an expansion of offshore drilling and he held a lease sale for offshore oil and gas leases in the Gulf of Mexico on August 2018.

April 28, 2017. President Trump signed an executive order repealing a ban on offshore drilling signed by President Obama and directing the Interior Secretary to review U.S. drilling policy and regulations.

The Trump administration curbed the burdensome Obama-era rule on methane, saving American energy developers hundreds of millions of dollars in regulatory costs.

Because of two proclamations, President Trump signed in December 2017 – which took effect in February 2018 – reducing the size of two national monuments in Utah, the lands were taken from the monuments were opened up for the states to decide what to do with it.

Fracking on federal lands increased because of Trump Administration policy changes.

As an illustration of the friendlier conditions for the coal industry under President Trump, an Alabama coal mine reopened because of confidence in his policies.

December 20, 2017. President Trump signed an executive order directing federal agencies to increase the production of important minerals that the U.S. is dependent on Chinese and Russian imports for, to order to reduce U.S. dependence on the countries.

October 24, 2018. The Trump Administration approved the first oil drilling permit for federal waters in the Arctic Ocean off Alaska.

April 10, 2019. President Trump signed two executive orders making it harder for states to block the construction of oil and gas pipelines, among other similar projects, because of environmental concerns.

April 25, 2019. The Trump Administration announced a plan to open up over one million acres of land in California to oil drilling, and it finalized this proposal on May 9, 2019 which cemented America's future for continued oil production.

May 15, 2019. The Trump Administration renewed two mineral leases for two sites in Minnesota, opening up those locations for copper mining after the Obama

Administration attempted to stop such plans.

September 12, 2019. The Trump Administration moved forward toward allowing oil and gas drilling and exploration in the Arctic National Wildlife Refuge.

September 15, 2019. President Trump authorized the use of the Strategic Petroleum Reserve after attacks on Saudi Arabia's oil facilities disrupted global oil markets.

September 18, 2019. President Trump announced his administration would revoke a federal waiver for California that allowed it to impose stricter auto emissions standards than the federal government. The Trump Administration officially revoked California's waiver the following day.

October 4, 2019. The Trump Administration announced it would open 725,000 acres of land in Central California to oil and gas drilling, ending a moratorium that had been in place since 2013.

October 4, 2019. The Trump Administration announced an ethanol plan to increase demand and benefit farmers.

October 9, 2019. The Trump Administration proposed relaxing regulations on mineral mining companies to make them more competitive.

October 15, 2019. The Trump Administration proposed allowing logging in the Tongass National Forest in Alaska.

October 22, 2019. The Trump Administration released a new scientific opinion changing protections on certain California fish to benefit farmers in the state reliant on water.

Trump's Courts And Judges.
Facts 534-544

President Trump is reshaping our Federal judiciary, appointing judges who will follow the Constitution as written. Over his first three years Trump has appointed 25% of all judges on the federal court of appeals.

With Judge Robert J Luck's appointment Trump flipped the 11th US Circuit Court of Appeals from mostly liberal to mostly conservative. This court includes the following, Middle District of Alabama, Northern District of Alabama, Southern District of Alabama, Middle District of Florida, Northern District of Florida, Southern District of Florida, Middle District of Georgia, Northern District of Georgia, and the Southern District of Georgia.

Trump was able to flip the US Court of Appeals for the 3rd circuit in March of 2019 to a mostly conservative court. This includes the District of Deaware, District of New Jersey, Eastern District of Pennsylvania, Middle District of Pennsylvania, and the Western District of Pennsylvania.

Through his appointments Trump has flipped the Court of Appeals 2nd Circuit. This court includes the districts of Connecticut, Eastern District of New York, Northern District of New York, Southern District of New York, Western District of New York, and the District of Vermont.

The 9th Circuit court which is the nation's largest appeals court has more judges appointed to it by Trump than any other president. The 9th Circuit comprises of California, Arizona, Alaska, Guam, Hawaii, Montana, Nevada, Idaho, the Northern Mariana Islands, Oregon, and Washington. Once the nation's most liberal court is now close to flipping conservative and if Trump gets another term in office it likely will.

In July 2018, President Trump broke the record for the most appeals court judges confirmed within his first two years when the Senate confirmed his 23rd nominee. The judges appointed by Trump and confirmed by the Senate wasted no time advancing an originalist and textualist philosophy. Textualism is an approach to the interpretation of statutes and the U.S. Constitution that focuses on the text itself and its plain meaning rather than inquiring into the purpose of those who wrote the text. Originalism is a method of constitutional interpretation that focuses on how a provision of a constitution would have been understood at the time of its ratification.

By 2019, Clarence Thomas, a strong originalist Supreme Court Justice, had become an influential figure, and by mid-2018, the Trump Administration had hired twenty-two of Thomas's former law clerks for executive branch positions and judgeships.

In March 17, 2017, the Trump administration notified the American Bar Association, which takes numerous left-wing positions and displays bias against conservatives, that it would end the ABA's role in evaluating judicial nominees before formally nominating them.

The President has appointed Circuit Court judges at a record pace and confirmed more circuit court judges than any other new administration. Trump has also been more consistent than any modern president in nominating conservatives and originalists to the judiciary.

President Trump has appointed two conservative

Supreme Court justices, Justice Neil Gorsuch and Justice Brett Kavanaugh.

On August 2019 Trump had his 150th judge confirmed.

Trump On Crime.
Facts 545-570

President Trump is cracking down on the MS-13 gang that has brought violence to communities across the country. In 2017, the DOJ worked with international partners to arrest and charge approximately 4,000 MS-13 members.

Because of Trump's policies US-Mexico border apprehensions have increased by 31.9%.

President Trump encouraged federal prosecutors to use the death penalty when possible in the fight against the trafficking of deadly drugs.

Trump launched an evaluation of grant programs to make sure the protection and safety of law enforcement officers was a priority.

Trump enhanced and updated the Project Safe Neighborhoods to help reduce violent crime.

Trump signed legislation making it easier to target websites that enable sex trafficking and strengthened penalties for people who promote or facilitate prostitution.

Trump created an interagency task force working around the clock to prosecute traffickers, protect victims, and prevent human trafficking.

Trump conducted Operation Cross Country XI to combat human trafficking, rescuing 84 children and arresting 120 human traffickers.

Trump signed an executive order directing the Attorney General to develop a strategy to more effectively prosecute people who commit crimes against law enforcement officers.

Trump advocated the death penalty for those who commit mass murders.

August 28, 2017. President Trump signed an executive order reversing Obama-era limitations on police departments' ability to buy surplus military equipment and re-establishing a program ended by the Obama Administration to help the police departments acquire the equipment.

President Trump kept his promise by launching the office of Victims of Immigration Crime Engagement (VOICE) within the Department of Homeland Security. Its directive is to support the victims and families affected by illegal alien crime; however, leftists took to pranking the phone line created, showing disrespect to the victims of illegal immigration.

President Trump appointed Noel Francisco, a strong conservative, as the U.S. Solicitor General, and the U.S. Senate confirmed him on September 19, 2017.

President Trump expressed strong support for the police and strong opposition to violence directed at police. Some law enforcement leaders described Trump as the biggest supporter of police in 2017 and argued that his support played a role in the reduction in anti-police violence that year. By May 2019, that year was on track to be the least deadly year for police officers since 1965.

President Trump gave $137 million in grants through the COPS Hiring Program to preserve jobs, increase community policing capacities, and support crime prevention efforts.

President Trump signed an executive order to focus more federal resources on dismantling transnational criminal organizations such as drug cartels.

February 9, 2017. President Trump signed an executive order for a strategy to be made for reducing crime in general, "including, in particular, illegal immigration, drug trafficking, and violent crime." Attorney General Sessions proceeded to implement the order.

December 21, 2018. President Trump signed the First Step Act, which includes bipartisan reforms to make our Federal justice system fairer and our communities safer. The First Step Act will help prepare inmates to successfully rejoin society, reducing recidivism and improving community safety. This legislation includes commonsense sentencing reforms that will make our Federal justice system fairer while keeping violent criminals and sex offenders off our streets. The First Step Act also reduced mandatory minimum sentences for certain crimes.

In April 2018, President Trump reportedly pledged not to crack down on marijuana in states with legalization laws and to support states' rights on the issue.

July 11, 2018. President Trump signed an executive order, which the DOJ implemented the same day, creating a multi-agency consumer fraud task force.

Law enforcement was one of the areas that President Trump prioritized when making political appointments, as seen by the fact that by December 2017, he was ahead of the Obama Administration in filling DOJ positions despite being behind overall.

President Trump called for a return to tough-on-crime policies, such as stop-and-frisk.

May 13, 2019. It was reported that Attorney General William Barr had appointed U.S. Attorney John Durham to investigate the origin of the Russian collusion hoax. On May 23, 2019, President Trump signed a memorandum ordering intelligence agencies to cooperate with Barr's investigation and giving the attorney general authority to declassify documents related to the 2016 surveillance of Trump's campaign.

March 13, 2019. President Trump criticized left-wing California governor Gavin Newsom for placing a moratorium on the state's death penalty despite voters approving of capital punishment in 2014 and 2016.

October 28, 2019. After giving a strong speech at the International Association of Chiefs of Police conference in Chicago, President Trump signed an executive order creating a commission to study crime and law enforcement and create recommendations on how to combat and reduce crime.

November 5, 2019. Trump signed a bill making animal cruelty a federal felony. The bipartisan bill, Preventing Animal Cruelty and Torture Act, criminalizes many acts of animal cruelty.

Trade Deals And Foreign Relations.
Facts 571-632

President Trump withdrew from the Paris Climate Agreement, which would have cost the U.S. nearly $3 trillion and led to 6.5 million fewer industrial sector jobs by 2040.

On April 30, 2018. the Trump Administration settled agreements with South Korea to enact quotas on steel imports from the country.

President Trump in his first year of office took a very strong stance on trade policy as president, and he recognized that America's previous leaders were to blame for the U.S. past trade failures, rather than other countries such as China.

President Trump did away with the North American Free Trade Agreement (NAFTA) and concluded a new U.S.-Mexico Trade Deal to replace it. Negotiations with Canada are currently underway to replace the old NAFTA trade deal.

The President renegotiated the United States–Korea Free Trade Agreement to preserve and grow jobs in the American auto industry and increase American exports.

President Trump reached a new agreement with the E.U. to increase U.S. exports. He agreed to work with the European Union towards zero tariffs, zero non-tariff barriers, and zero subsides.

Trump is confronting China's unfair trade practices after

years of Washington looking the other way.

March 8, 2018. President Trump, through two orders using Section 232 of the Trade Expansion Act of 1962, imposed a 25% tariff on all steel imports and a 10% tariff on all aluminum imports, something he did both for economic and national security reasons. Canada, Mexico, the European Union, and six other U.S. allies were excluded when the tariffs went into effect pending further trade deal negotiations.

Liberal news outlets called Trump "unhinged" when he called himself the chosen one but they left out the context, Trump was talking about how the people of the United States chose him to make good trade deals.

After an investigation into Chinese forced technology transfers, unfair licensing practices, and intellectual property theft president Trump held China accountable for its unfair trade practices by imposing tariffs on $250 billion in Chinese goods.

January 22, 2018. President Trump imposed tariffs on solar energy products and washing machine imports, using a section of U.S. trade law last used early in George W. Bush's presidency.

On August 1, 2018. President Trump directed the USTR to consider raising the proposed $200 billion tariff rates to 25% from 10%. On August 7, 2018, the Trump Administration finalized 25% tariffs on $16 billion worth of Chinese imports, with the tariffs going into effect later that month. On September 17, 2018, the Trump Administration announced it would increase tariffs on another $200 billion worth of Chinese imports from 10% to 25% pending the two countries negotiating a new trade deal. The tariff increase ultimately was implemented on May 10, 2019. That same day, the USTR began the process of raising tariffs on all remaining Chinese imports.

April 19, 2018. President Trump signed an executive order that, among other changes, loosened U.S. regulations on arms exports to foreign countries and sped up the approval process for weapons sales, including those for military drones. The State Department's proposed implementation plan for the new rules were finalized and began being implemented in February of 2019.

North Korean vice-foreign minister stated Trump's foreign policy was "more vicious and more aggressive" than that of Barack Obama.

April 20, 2017. President Trump signed a memorandum directing the Department of Commerce to investigate whether steel imports pose a threat to U.S. national security.

April 25, 2017. After Canada changed its milk pricing policy, putting U.S. farmers at a severe disadvantage, the Trump Administration imposed tariffs at rates up to 24% on Canadian lumber imports.

April 27, 2017. President Trump signed a memorandum opening a Department of Commerce investigation into whether the high level of aluminum imports constitutes a threat to U.S. national security.

May 11, 2017. President Trump approved a trade deal with China which would increase American exports.

American beef exports have returned to China for the first time in more than a decade. June 12, 2017, The U.S. and China made an agreement that would allow American beef products to be exported to China which began entering China soon afterward. A month later China allowed the U.S. to export rice to the nation.

Among President Trump's 2017 foreign policy achievements: Leaving or announcing intention to leave globalist agreements, including the UN Population Fund, Global Compact on Migration, Paris Climate Agreement and UNESCO, and giving a strong pro-sovereignty speech at the UN General Assembly.

Among President Trump's 2018 foreign policy achievements: Leaving or announcing intention to leave the United Nations Human Rights Council, Global Compact for Refugees, Iran Nuclear Deal, Universal Postal Union, and taking a tough stance against the International Criminal Court.

August 8, 2017. The Trump Administration placed a punitive import tax on Chinese aluminum foil imports after a preliminary determination that the country was illegally dumping the product into the U.S. Then in February of 2018 Department of Commerce upheld the tariffs and raised their rates.

November 30, 2017. The Trump Administration formally opposed giving China market economy status in the World Trade Organization.

Trump secured $250 billion in new trade and investment

deals in China and $12 billion in Vietnam.

Trump made a deal with the European Union to increase U.S. energy exports like that of liquefied natural gas.

Trump secured access to new markets for America's farmers such as the deal with Mexico which included new improvements enabling food and agriculture to trade more fairly.

Trump's agreement with the E.U. will reduce barriers and increase the trade of American soybeans to Europe.

Trump litigated multiple WTO (World Trade Organization) disputes targeting unfair trade practices and upholding our right to enact fair trade laws such as a dispute with Indonesia's unfair restriction of U.S. agricultural exports.

Trump defended American Tuna fishermen and packagers before the WTO.

President Trump has established a Trade and Investment Working Group to lay the groundwork for post-Brexit trade with the United Kingdom.

The Administration authorized $12 billion to aid farmers affected by unfair retaliatory tariffs.

Trump opened up Argentina to American pork experts for the first time in a quarter-century.

March 31, 2017. President Trump signed an executive order to institute a crack down on violations of anti-dumping laws and help to officials to collect penalties already owed to the U.S. Over the next two years Trump would continue to crackdown on countries dumping items such as aluminum foil, washing machines, kegs, and a half dozen others mostly coming from China. He also imposed safeguard tariffs to protect domestic washing machines and solar products manufacturers hurt by China's trade policies.

March 31, 2017. President Trump signed an executive order that ordered a report by the Department of Commerce and the U.S. Trade Representative on the causes of the U.S. trade deficit due within 90 days.

American steel and aluminum jobs are coming back following President Trump's tariffs with U.S. steel mills seeing a nearly 5% shipment increase in 2018. U.S. Steel announced in August 2018 that it would invest $750 million in its Gary, Indiana, plant, crediting the steel tariffs. U.S. Steel then announced it would increase operations in Granite City, Illinois and announced they would restart construction of a plant in Alabama, something the company credited President Trump's tariffs for. On May 2, 2019, U.S. Steel announced it would invest over $1 billion in its plants near Pittsburgh. Nucor announced it would build a new steel mill in Florida then the next year Nucor announced that because of President Trump's tariffs, it would invest $1.3 billion to build a new steel mill in the Midwest. JSW announced it would invest $500 million to build a new steel plant in Ohio, something it announced after announcing an additional $500 million investment in an existing plant in Texas. Braidy Industries moved forward in building a new aluminum mill that would create 550 new jobs. Steel Dynamics announced it would invest up to $1.8 billion to build a new steel mill in the southwest

U.S. that would create about 600 jobs. And in January 2019, Republic Steel announced it would reopen a steel mill in Ohio. The CPA estimated that 2.1 million jobs were created in 2018 by Trump's steel tariffs and its other economic policies.

Once enacted by Congress, Trump's United States–Mexico–Canada Agreement (USMCA) will incentivize billions of dollars in auto and auto parts production in the United States and create a freer and fairer market for American agriculture. USMCA also includes the strongest-ever provisions on labor, environmental, digital, and intellectual property protections to reflect the realities of the 21st-century economy.

The Trump Administration, in an effort to save U.S. jobs, reached agreements with Qatar and the United Arab Emirates in a dispute over the two countries subsidizing their airlines.

May 23, 2018. At the request of President Trump, the Commerce Department began an investigation into whether auto imports pose a national security threat to the U.S. The department formally delivered the results of the report to President Trump on February 17, 2019.

July 18, 2018. The Commerce Department announced it would investigate whether uranium imports threaten U.S. national security. In a decision made on July 12, 2019, President Trump declined to establish uranium import quotas, though he did acknowledge that the Commerce Department's findings "raise significant concerns" and ordered a deeper review by a working group to make recommendations.

August 10, 2018. President Trump announced the U.S. would double its aluminum and steel tariffs against Turkey, coming during a dispute over Turkey's detainment of an American pastor in the country as well as the devaluing of Turkey's Lira currency. On May 16, 2019, President Trump signed a proclamation reducing the steel tariff back to 25%, citing its success in reducing Turkey's exports to the U.S., and he also ended the country's preferential trade status.

August 23, 2018. President Trump signed a memorandum making it U.S. policy to end international mail discounts created by a UN agency which made it cheaper to send a product to the U.S. from a foreign country than from a location inside the United States. On October 17, 2018, the Trump Administration formally announced it would begin the process of withdrawing from the Universal Postal Union within the next year to negotiate fair international postal rates for American mailers.

September 24, 2018. President Trump signed a revised trade agreement that his administration renegotiated with South Korea's president. The agreement did not require U.S. Senate approval, and South Korea's parliament ratified it on December 7, 2018.

December 1, 2018. In the G-20's statement, the Trump administration succeeded in calling for World Trade Organization reform and removing a statement against protectionism.

April 26, 2018. President Trump declared this day to be World Intellectual Property Day, stating that "our country will no longer turn a blind eye to the theft of American jobs, wealth, and intellectual property through the unfair and unscrupulous economic practices of some foreign actors."

Through his trade actions, President Trump helped revive the GOP's historical support for tariffs. By 2018, blue-collar manufacturing towns in the U.S. that had once supported Democrats had become strongly Republican, largely because of the GOP's and Trump's increasingly tough stance on trade issues.

Because of Trump's tariffs, exports rose 6.6% in May 2018, causing the United States' trade deficit to drop to the lowest level since October 2016.

Despite fears that President Trump's tariffs would do the opposite, by August 2018 prospective military sales to U.S. allies reached $63 billion – 50% higher than in 2017. By July 2018, the U.S. had already sold more weapons that year than the entire year in 2017, and in Fiscal Year 2018, the dollar value of U.S. arms sales nearly reached the record set in 2012. The State Department reported in November 2018 that U.S. arms sales increased 13% in Fiscal Year 2018 compared to the previous year, with arms sales specifically from the U.S. government to a foreign government increasing 33% during the same period.

January 31, 2019. President Trump signed an executive order directing federal agencies to favor contractors who use American-made materials in construction projects.

February 27, 2019. In Vietnam, President Trump presided over the signing of several trade deals worth $21 billion between U.S. and Vietnamese companies that would support an estimated 83,000 American jobs.

March 4, 2019. The Trump Administration announced it would end preferential trade status for India and Turkey since such treatment had not led to any advantages to the

U.S. On May 16, 2019, President Trump signed a proclamation making the termination for Turkey official. On May 31, 2019, the Trump Administration announced it would end India's special status on June 5, 2019.

April 3, 2019. President Trump signed a memorandum cracking down on online counterfeit goods trafficking on websites such as Amazon and eBay.

April 8, 2019. The Trump Administration proposed a list of $11 billion worth of tariffs on European Union products in retaliation against the EU's subsidies for Airbus. On July 1, 2019, the USTR proposed an additional $4 billion in tariffs because of the Airbus subsidies.

May 7, 2019. Trump reimposed a 17.5% tariff on tomatoes from Mexico after the U.S. withdrew from a 2013 agreement suspending the tariff.

May 23, 2019. Trump had the Commerce Department propose imposing tariffs on any country that artificially devalues its currency.

July 2, 2019. Trump imposed 456% tariffs on South Korean and Taiwanese steel transshipped through Vietnam to avoid existing U.S. tariffs.

July 15, 2019. President Trump signed an executive order significantly increasing the required percentages of American components in materials used for government projects.

July 26, 2019. President Trump signed a memorandum directing the USTR to do everything in its power to prevent the WTO from allowing countries to claim "developing country" status within the organization if they have strong economies that make such a designation unnecessary.

August 5, 2019. The Trump Administration formally labeled China a currency manipulator, the first time the U.S. government had officially done so since 1994 and fulfilling a 2016 campaign promise.

Trump signs the US-Japan trade deal on October 7th. Japan is the world's third-biggest economy behind the United States and China. The deal reportedly will most benefit American farmers as 11 other Pacific Rim countries were getting preferential treatment in Japan before the deal.

October 25, 2019. President Trump signed a proclamation restoring preferential trade status to Ukraine after its government took action to satisfy U.S. intellectual property concerns, and he also removed some imports from Thailand from the program.

October 31, 2019. President Trump announced he would end some trade benefits for Cameroon because of human rights abuses in the country.

President Trump signed two bills in support of Hong Kong's pro-democracy movement. In response, Hong Kong protesters held a Thanksgiving rally and held up images of Donald Trump's face photoshopped onto Rocky Balboa's muscular body.

National Defense.
Facts 633-699

President Trump ended the defense cuts of the past Administration and has secured historic investments to rebuild our military. President Trump signed legislation providing $700 billion for defense in 2018 and $716 billion in 2019.

President Trump is supporting America's men and women in uniform by securing the largest military pay raise in nearly a decade.

The President issued a new National Security Strategy to keep America safe from all threats. The Administration has also released new strategies specific to cybersecurity, counterterrorism, and weapons of mass destruction terrorism. He also released America's first fully articulated cyber strategy in 15 years and a new strategy on national bio-defense, which better prepares the nation to defend against biological threats.

In 2019 Trump called off peace negotiations with the President of Afghanistan after they admitted to an attack in Kabul that killed an American soldier.

The President's leadership encouraged the North Atlantic Treaty Organization (NATO) allies to increase defense spending to their agreed-upon levels. In 2017 alone, there was an increase of more than 4.8 percent in defense spending amongst NATO allies. Every member state has increased defense spending.

Because of Trump, eight NATO allies increased defense

spending and will reach the agreed-upon 2 percent benchmark by the end of 2018 and 15 allies are on trade to do so by 2024. NATO allies spent over 42 billion dollars more on defense from 2016 to 2019.

President Trump convinced the Alliance to strengthen counterterrorism activities, and NATO formally joined the coalition to defeat ISIS.

President Trump has imposed tough sanctions on the corrupt regimes in Venezuela, Cuba, and Nicaragua.

In addition to sanctions, Trump imposed strong sanctions on Venezuelan dictator Nicholas Maduro and his inner circle.

President Trump signed an executive order preventing those in the U.S. from carrying out certain transactions with the Venezuelan regime, including prohibiting the purchase of the regime's debt.

The Trump administration has enhanced support for Ukraine's defense by stepping up sales of weapons to its military.

Trump expelled dozens of Russian intelligence officers from the United States and ordered the closure of the Russian consulate in Seattle, WA.

February 3, 2017. The Trump administration and Lockheed Martin reached a tentative deal that would purchase 90 F-35 jets at the lowest price in the program's history. The first 90 planes were about $725 million below budget, with billions of more dollars of savings expected, and it saved at least one U.S. ally, Japan, $100 million. Then on May 10, 2019, the Pentagon signed a deal with Lockheed Martin over a major F-35 Lightning II that reduced the price by 8.8%.

The Trump administration gave wider powers to the Department of Defense than it had under Obama. In April 2017, President Trump gave Mattis authority to set troop levels in Iraq and Syria for the fight against ISIS, and it gave military commanders the authority to perform military actions without approval from Washington. The U.S. military made large advances against ISIS under their autonomy. In June 2017, the Trump Administration authorized the Defense Department to set troop levels in Afghanistan, and in October 2017, it relaxed the rules of engagement for its troops in the country by ending a requirement for soldiers to be in contact with the enemy before opening fire. The expanded authority given to the military could also be seen in U.S. operations in Somalia.

Trump was very pleased that Defense Secretary James Mattis ordered a department-wide review of its military training requirements, particularly that which is irrelevant to actual war-fighting such as political correctness exercises, to make the military more effective and lethal.

President Trump directed the first whole-of-government assessment of United States manufacturing and defense supply chains since the Eisenhower administration.

President Trump initiated the 2018 Nuclear Posture Review, improving United States deterrence policy and existing capabilities to counter nuclear threats.

President Trump empowered our military commanders with broad authority to take the fight to ISIS, and the results are clear. ISIS has lost nearly all of its territory, more than half of which has been liberated since President Trump took office. All of ISIS' territory in Iraq was successfully liberated. ISIS' self-proclaimed capital city Raqqah has been recaptured. ISIS' territorial caliphate has been defeated.

By the end of 2017, ISIS lost 98% of the territory it once held, and most all of its losses occurred during the Trump administration.

President Trump announced a new Iran strategy to confront all of Iran's malign activities and withdrew from the one-sided Iran nuclear deal. All sanctions that had been lifted or waived under the Iran deal have been reimposed. Withdrew from Iran deal and immediately began the process of re-imposing sanctions that had been lifted or waived. All nuclear-related sanctions will be back in full force by early November 2018.

January 30, 2018. President Trump signed an executive order to keep Guantanamo Bay Detention Camp open – reversing an order signed by Obama in 2009. As stated in the order, on May 2, 2018, the Pentagon announced that Defense Secretary Mattis had sent new criteria to the White House for when to send individuals to Guantanamo.

July 2, 2018. The Trump administration moved to block China Mobile from expanding operations to the U.S., recommending the FCC to reject its application.

August 13, 2018. President Trump signed the 2019 National Defense Authorization Act into law, which, among other reforms, banned the U.S. government from using products from the Chinese companies ZTE and Huawei, strengthened the Committee on Foreign Investment in the United States (CFIUS), took measures to counter Chinese government influence in domestic U.S. society, and allowed Defense Secretary Mattis to waive sanctions on countries that had bought Russian weapons in the past but now wanted to buy American weapons. While the bill took a tough stance on China, some of its measures were more lenient than originally proposed.

October 11, 2018. The Trump administration enacted restrictions on nuclear technology exports to China to prevent the country from using those exports to strengthen its military.

October 24, 2018. Trump's Defense Secretary issued a memo creating a task force to find ways to protect the U.S. defense supply chain and prevent China, Russia, and other enemies from stealing important technologies. The following January, President Trump signed four memorandums to strengthen the U.S. defense supply.

October 4, 2018. The Trump administration released its counterterrorism strategy, the first one since 2011. The strategy strongly differed from the Obama Administration's policies, and it emphasized targeting "radical Islamic terrorist groups."

September 11, 2018. In his proclamation commemorating the September 11, 2001 attacks, President Trump condemned the "radical Islamist terrorists" who conducted the attacks.

February 11, 2019. President Trump signed an executive order creating a national strategy for artificial intelligence and ordering federal agencies to prioritize AI development and to protect American AI technology from getting into the wrong hands, among other provisions.

March 15, 2019. President Trump signed an executive order that updated a 2011 order signed by President Obama, strengthening the definition of a "significant transnational criminal organization" so that the Trump Administration could better counter Mexican cartels and other similar organizations.

March 26, 2019. President Trump signed an executive order that took several steps to protect the U.S. and its electric grid from an EMP attack.

April 17, 2019. The Trump administration ended the Obama-era practice of disclosing the size of the U.S. nuclear weapon stockpile.

June 21, 2019. In a series of tweets, Trump explains that he canceled a retaliatory attack on Iran in response to an American drone getting shot down. The president writes that he called off the strike after being told that 150 people could have been killed, reasoning that the response was not proportional since the downed American aircraft was unmanned.

The Trump administration has also rolled out sanctions targeting those tied to Syria's chemical weapons program.

President Trump elevated the Department of Defense's Cyber Command to the status of Unified Combatant Command, showing the Trump Administration's increased focus on cybersecurity. May 11, 2017, President Trump signed an executive order to review U.S. cybersecurity and hold the various federal departments accountable for ensuring the protection of valuable information.

November 16, 2018. President Trump signed a bill into law making the Department of Homeland Security the most important agency for cybersecurity and organizing the agency's cybersecurity division.

August 15, 2018. President Trump signed an order reversing an Obama-era directive limiting how the U.S. can launch cyberattacks against foreign nations. On September 20, 2018, the Trump administration announced it had implemented a new national cyber strategy.

May 2, 2019. President Trump signed an executive order intended to improve the federal government's cybersecurity workforce.

July 11, 2017. The Trump administration limited the governmental use of Kaspersky Lab software due to suspicions that the Russian government was using it for cyber espionage. The Trump Administration ordered the full removal of the software from government computers in September 2017. On December 12, 2017, President Trump signed into law a ban on Kaspersky Lab software in the U.S. government.

July 21, 2017. President Trump signed an executive order requiring a government-wide review of the U.S. defense industry to improve national security, described as one of the most significant such reviews since Dwight D. Eisenhower's presidency. On October 5, 2018, the Trump administration released the review's findings and took action based on those findings.

September 13, 2017. The Trump administration blocked

the purchase of a U.S. superconductor maker firm to a Chinese company supported by the nation's government. This was the fourth time in 27 years that a U.S. president had blocked a foreign takeover of an American company.

October 26, 2017. The Trump administration instituted tougher security screenings for people flying to the U.S.

April 13, 2017. Under the increased autonomy President Trump gave the Defense Department, the U.S. dropped a GBU-43B (also known as MOAB or the "Mother Of All bombs"), the largest nonnuclear bomb in existence at 21,000 pounds on a complex of Islamic State tunnels in Afghanistan. Although tested in 2003, the bomb had never been used in combat before. It caused much damage, is estimated to have killed at least 94 ISIS fighters, including four commanders – no civilians were killed. It also destroyed several of the tunnels as well as weapon stockpiles. The attack was reported as having dealt a heavy blow to ISIS's Afghanistan branch.

Unlike former President Obama, the State Department under President Trump described the Afghanistan Taliban as a terrorist organization without hesitation.

The President announced that the Department of Defense will work to create a Space Force to serve as an independent branch of the United States military.

President Trump held a historic summit with Chairman Kim Jong-Un, bringing beginnings of peace and denuclearization to the Korean Peninsula. Because of the President's actions, North Korea has halted nuclear and missile tests.

Before the summit with Kim Jong-un, President Trump's

leadership helped secure the passage of historic UN sanctions on North Korea.

June 30, 2019. Trump becomes the first sitting president to enter North Korea. He takes 18 steps beyond the border and shakes hands with Kim.

Trump negotiated with North Korea for them to return the remains of missing-in-action soldiers from the Korean War.

President Trump withdrew the United States from the UN Human Rights Council due to its bias against Israel.

Trump has made clear that he does not accept the International Criminal Court's jurisdiction over Americans and will continue to protect America's sovereignty. And his administration has announced that it will use whatever means necessary to protect American citizens and servicemen from unjust prosecution by the International Criminal Court.

In responded to the use of chemical weapons by the Syrian regime against its civilians, Trump rolled out sanctions targeting individuals and entities tied to Syria's chemical weapons program. He then directed strikes in April 2017 against a Syrian airfield used in a chemical weapons attack on innocent civilians. Trump also joined allies in launching airstrikes in April 2018 against targets associated with Syria's chemical weapons use.

A new Cuba policy that enhanced compliance with U.S. law and held the Cuban regime accountable for political oppression and human rights abuses. Directed by Trump, the Treasury and State are working to channel economic activity away from the Cuban regime, particularly the military.

President Trump has successfully advocated for cutting waste at the UN. Changes made to the organization's structure allowed the UN to cut hundreds of millions of dollars from its budget while making the organization more efficient.

May 15, 2018. President Trump signed an executive order strengthening the chief information officer role in federal agencies in order to modernize and improve the information technology at those agencies.

On August 15, 2018 the Trump administration revoked the security clearance of anti-Trump commentator and former CIA director John Brennan. This came after the Trump Administration announced it was considering revoking the security clearances of several former Obama Administration officials who had criticized the president or become political pundits.

In a historic show of transparency and accountability, the Trump administration completed the Department of Defense's first-ever audit.

May 15, 2019. President Trump signed an executive order empowering the U.S. government to block foreign tech companies from operating in the U.S. if they pose a national security threat. Shortly after the order's signing, the Commerce Department placed Huawei and seventy affiliates on its "Entity List," meaning it could no longer buy parts in the U.S. without federal government approval. On June 29, 2019, President Trump announced he would allow U.S. companies to sell to Huawei as part of an agreement to restart trade negotiations with China.

By mid-2019, the Trump Administration had significantly slowed its approvals of semiconductor company requests to hire Chinese citizens for sensitive positions.

President Trump has taken tough action to combat Russia's malign activities, including Russia's efforts to undermine United States elections. The Administration has imposed sanctions on more than 200 individuals and entities related to Russia's destabilizing activities. Imposed sanctions against five Russian entities and three individuals for enabling Russia's military and intelligence units to increase Russia's offensive cyber capabilities. Sanctions against seven Russian oligarchs, and 12 companies they own or control, who profit from Russia's destabilizing activities. Sanctioned 100 targets in response to Russia's occupation of Crimea and aggression in Eastern Ukraine.

July 22, 2019. President Trump ordered the Defense Department to find better ways to obtain rare earth minerals, something done to lessen U.S. dependence on China.

The Trump administration has secured the release of numerous American citizens held abroad, including Pastor Andrew Brunson from Turkey, Josh Holt from Venezuela, and more. More than a dozen American hostages have been freed from captivity across the world that Obama could or would do nothing about.

President Trump attended G20 summits in Argentina and Germany, where he promoted American First policies and encouraged closer cooperation.

Trump signed an executive order to help military spouses find employment as their families deploy domestically and abroad.

June 30, 2017. The Department of Defense announced it would delay an Obama Administration plan to have the military recruit transgender people for six months to ensure the military's readiness would not be affected by the change. On July 26, 2017, President Trump announced he would reverse Obama's policy and disallow transgender people from serving in the military, and he formally signed an order banning them from joining the military on August 25, 2017. President Trump signed a final order on March 23, 2018.

In 2019 Trump named retired Navy SEAL Admiral Joseph Maguire the nation's top intelligence position.

September 10, 2019. President Trump signed an executive order allowing the federal government to impose sanctions on terrorist leaders without needing to specify specific actions committed by those individuals.

October 27, 2019. President Trump announced that ISIS leader Abu Bakr al-Baghdadi had been killed by U.S. forces one day earlier. When he released the news he said of Baghdadi, "He died after running into a dead-end tunnel, whimpering and crying and screaming all the way." Trump also tweeted a picture of the American service dog that chased him down the tunnel.

Trump's Love For Veterans.
Facts 700-729

The VA Choice and Quality Employment Act that Trump signed in 2017 authorized $2.1 billion in additional funds for the Veterans Choice Program. In september the VA announced it had exceeded its goal of delivering 81,000 appeals decisions in the Fiscal Year 2018, a 52% increase from 2017, on claims for disability benefits two weeks earlier than expected.

President Trump secured a record $73.1 billion in funding for the Department of Veterans Affairs to provide quality medical care for our veterans. This funding included $8.6 billion for mental health services, $400 million for opioid abuse prevention, $206 million for suicide prevention, and more.

Trump increased transparency and accountability at the VA by launching an online "Access and Quality Tool," providing veterans with access to wait-time and quality of care data.

President Trump and his Administration have expanded access to telehealth services for veterans, including through the "Anywhere to Anywhere" VA health care initiative making it easier for veterans to obtain health care services such as by letting them conduct medical examinations remotely and giving them the ability to schedule appointments electronically.

Trump signed the Veterans Treatment Court Improvement Act, increasing the number of VA employees that can assist justice-involved veterans.

President Trump issued an executive order requiring the Administration to improve access to mental health treatment resources for veterans.

President Trump signed an executive order requiring the Secretaries of Defense, Homeland Security, and Veterans Affairs to submit a joint plan to provide veterans access to mental health treatment as they transition to civilian life.

March 5, 2019. President Trump signed an order creating a task force to combat and reduce veteran suicides.

President Trump signed the Veterans Affairs Accountability and Whistleblower Protection Act, making it easier to fire failing employees and protect whistleblowers. Under President Trump, the VA has removed, demoted, or suspended more than 4,300 employees for poor performance. Strengthened protections for individuals who come forward and identify programs occurring within the VA.

President Trump signed the Veterans Appeals Improvement and Modernization Act of 2017, streamlining the process used by veterans when appealing benefits claims.

Trump's VA MISSION Act enacted sweeping reform to the VA system that: Consolidated and strengthened VA community care programs. Funding for the Veterans Choice program. Expanded eligibility for the Family Caregivers Program. Gave veterans more access to walk-in care. Strengthened the VA's ability to recruit and retain quality healthcare professionals. This also enabled the VA to modernize its assets and infrastructure.

Trump worked to shift veterans' electronic medical records to the same system used by the Department of Defense, a decades-old priority.

President Trump fulfilled his promise to create a White House VA Hotline to help veterans and principally staffed it with veterans and direct family members of veterans.

The President signed the Forever GI Bill, providing veterans, service members, and their families with enhanced education benefits.

Trump signed the Harry W. Colmery Veterans Educational Assistance Act, providing enhanced educational benefits to veterans, service members, and their family members. This also lifted a 15-year limit on veterans' access to their educational benefits.

Trump signed legislation that provided $86.5 billion in funding for the Department of Veterans Affairs, the largest dollar amount in history for the VA.

June 2, 2017. President Trump signed a bill into law giving preference in federal grants to "federal and state law enforcement agencies that hire and train veterans".

August 12, 2017. President Trump signed a bill which, in addition to extending the department's Choice Program for an additional six months, authorized $1.8 billion so the VA could lease and open 28 medical facilities and so it could implement a new hiring program.

August 23, 2017. President Trump signed a bill into law streamlining and making more convenient the process for veterans to appeal disability benefit claims.

September 18, 2018. Because of Trump's actions, the VA announced that five of its hospitals were removed from its list of high-risk facilities because of improving conditions.

The Trump Administration continued working to reduce the number of homeless veterans, and the number fell over 5% between 2017 and 2018 and stood at half the level in 2009, with female veteran homelessness falling 10% between 2017 and 2018.

June 25, 2019. President Trump signed a bill into law that fast-tracked benefits for Vietnam veterans likely exposed to Agent Orange.

Rather than holding a press conference after his first foreign trip, President Trump gave a speech to U.S. soldiers.

March 4, 2019. President Trump signed an executive order to help veterans and active-duty service members easily join the U.S. Merchant Marine.

July 1, 2017. President Trump held a "Celebrate Freedom Rally" in Washington D.C. to honor veterans and celebrate Independence Day– his first Independence Day address as President. In it, he spoke again strongly in favor of religious liberty and stated that "since the signing of the Declaration of Independence 241 years ago, America always affirmed that liberty comes from our creator. Our rights are given to us by God, and no earthly force can ever take those rights away."

July 4, 2019. To celebrate Independence Day, President Trump held a "Salute to America" rally at the Lincoln Memorial, an event that honored the U.S. armed forces and which included several military flyovers along with tanks and armored vehicles. Trump gave a strongly patriotic speech that honored and celebrated American history, and he also honored Border Patrol and ICE officials.

Through an executive order, President Trump forgave all student loan debt for about 25,000 permanently disabled Veterans.

November 11, 2019. President Trump became the first president to attend the New York City Veterans Day Parade, attending and speaking on its 100th anniversary.

November 15, 2019. President Trump pardoned two members of the U.S. Military, Clint Lorance and Mathew Golsteyn and then defied the Navy and restored the rank of U.S. Navy SEAL Eddie Gallagher who was exonerated of charges.

Thanksgiving day 2019, Newsweek released a story about how Trump was going to be spending the holiday playing golf and tweeting. President didn't take the day off however, he traveled 13 hours by flight to Afghanistan the night before on a surprise visit to spend Thanksgiving with the troops. Trump told the troops, "There's nowhere I'd rather celebrate this Thanksgiving than right here with the toughest, strongest, best and bravest warriors on the face of the Earth."

Fighting the Opioid Crisis.
Facts 730-747

January 10, 2017. President Trump signed the Interdict Act into law, which provided $9 million for Customs and Border Protection so it could buy equipment to help it stop the flow of fentanyl and other opioids through the country's borders.

On October 24, 2018. President Trump signed the STOP Act into law as part of a major bill to combat the opioids crisis, which improved cooperation between the CBP and the United States Postal Service to crack down on illegal fentanyl imports.

The President helped secure a record $6 billion in funding to fight the opioid epidemic.

The President launched a national public awareness campaign about the dangers of opioid addiction and youth opioid usage.

The U.S has reduced high-dose opioid prescriptions by 16 percent during Trump's first year in office.

In 2018, President Trump created a Commission on Combating Drug Addiction and the Opioid Crisis, which recommends ways to tackle the opioid crisis.

The President signed the landmark Support for Patients and Communities Act, the largest and most comprehensive legislative package addressing a single drug crisis in history.

June 28, 2018. As part of President Trump's

administration's efforts to address the opioid epidemic, the DOJ charged 601 people in the largest ever health care fraud enforcement action.

The Administration declared the opioid crisis a nationwide Public Health Emergency in 2017 and because of President Trump's policies that went along with that, in 2018 Opioid deaths in Iowa went down 33%.

Trump led two National Prescription Drug Take-Back Days in 2017 and 2018, collecting a record number of expired and unneeded prescription drugs each time.

Trump gave out $485 million targeted grants in fiscal year 2017 to help areas hit hardest by the opioid crisis.

Trump had the DOJ launch a Joint Criminal Opioid Darknet Enforcement (J-CODE) team, aimed at disrupting online illicit opioid sales.

President Trump signed INTERDICT Act, strengthening efforts to detect and intercept synthetic opioids before they reach our communities.

To help raise awareness about the human toll of the opioid crisis Trump brought the "Prescribed to Death" memorial to President's Park near the White House.

President Trump chaired meeting the 73rd General Session of the United Nations discussing the worldwide drug problem with international leaders.

The President launched a Safer Prescribing Plan that seeks to cut nationwide opioid prescription fills by one-third within three years.

October 23, 2018. The Trump Administration began a program to help mothers and babies affected by opioids.

Trump donated his 2019 third-quarter salary to help tackle the nation's opioid epidemic and gave it to the Assistant Secretary of Health.

Trump On Healthcare.
Facts 748-772

President Trump's Administration is working to provide Americans with affordable alternatives to Obamacare. The Administration expanded short-term, limited-duration health insurance plans that are expected to be nearly 50 percent cheaper than unsubsidized Obamacare plans.

President Trump has expanded association health plans, allowing more employers to join together across State lines and affordably offer coverage to their employees.

Americans have more healthcare freedom thanks to the President signing legislation that ended Obamacare's individual mandate penalty.

While healthcare premiums had been steadily increasing as a result of Obamacare, the average benchmark exchange premium will decline for the first time in 2019 thanks to President Trump's policies.

President Trump signed the most comprehensive childhood cancer legislation ever into law, which will advance childhood cancer research and improve treatments.

President Trump enacted changes to the Medicare 340B program, saving seniors an estimated $320 million on drugs in 2018 alone.

President Trump signed legislation eliminating contractual gag clauses that stopped pharmacists from informing patients about lower drug prices.

President Trump signed "Right to Try" legislation to expand access to experimental treatments for terminally ill patients.

President Trump released a blueprint to drive down drug prices for American patients, leading multiple major drug companies to announce they will freeze or reverse price increases. This has led to the largest decrease in prescription drug prices in 51 years according to the Council of Economic Advisors.

October 12, 2017. President Trump signed an executive order to increase market competition and make the healthcare market freer, such as by expanding access to plans that reach across state lines and which do not have to comply with ObamaCare rules.

June 5, 2019. The Trump Administration announced it would end research at the National Institutes of Health that uses fetal tissue, and it also ended government funding to a university for such research. The HHS also announced that it would conduct ethics reviews before funding private research projects.

October 1, 2017. Trump became the first president since Bill Clinton in 1993 to recognize Down Syndrome Awareness Month. One year later President Trump recognized Down Syndrome Awareness Month again issuing a pro-life statement that condemned Down syndrome-selective abortions. He did so again the next year inviting several individuals with Down syndrome and their families to the White House.

November 2017. President Trump proclaimed this month National Adoption Month, stating that "no child in America —born or unborn—is unwanted or unloved."

March 18, 2019. Trump Administration announced it would overhaul FEMA's flood insurance program.

July 10, 2018. The Trump Administration announced it would cut funding for Obamacare outreach from $36.8 million to $10 million – the funding was at $62.5 million before the Trump Administration began cutting it in 2017.

Trump signed legislation to improve the National Suicide Hotline.

October 22, 2018. The Trump administration proposed a rule to allow employers to contribute to cheaper health reimbursement arrangements, reversing an Obama-era regulation. The administration released the finalized version of this rule on June 13, 2019.

November 13, 2018. The Trump Administration gave more flexibility to the states to provide inpatient mental health treatment for individuals.

November 29, 2018. The Trump Administration announced four ways it would give waivers to the states so they could receive federal subsidies for health care plans that do not meet Obamacare's requirements.

May 11, 2018. President Trump announced his plan to lower drug prices further, which he did while criticizing the drug industry and foreign governments for its practices that hurt American citizens.

July 10, 2019. President Trump signed an executive order

to improve kidney disease care, including making it easier to obtain transplants and in-home dialysis, as well as taking steps to lower prices.

July 31, 2019. The Trump administration announced two new proposals to lower drug prices, including allowing drug imports from Canada.

On September 30th Trump signed the Autism CARES Bill into law saying, "You are not forgotten, we are fighting for you!" The bill provides 1.8 billion dollars for autism research and services.

September 19, 2019. President Trump signed an executive order to help develop better vaccines against seasonal influenza and a potential flu pandemic.

October 3, 2019. President Trump signed an executive order strengthening and giving a more prominent role to Medicare Advantage, a privately-operated section of Medicare.

Trump's Pro-Life Agenda.
Facts 773-796

President Trump defunded a United Nations agency for colluding with China's program of forced abortion and sterilization.

April 13, 2017. President Trump signed a Congressional Review bill into law annulling a recent Obama administration regulation that would have prohibited states from discriminating in awarding Title X family planning funds based on whether the local clinic also performs abortions (some states adopted rules which distribute federal family planning funds on the condition that the organizations do not perform abortions). The Act was called "the first major national pro-life bill in more than a decade."

President Trump overturned the Obama administration's midnight regulation prohibiting states from defunding certain abortion facilities.

Trump favored modifying the 2016 Republican platform opposing abortion, to allow for exceptions in cases of rape, incest, and circumstances endangering the health of the mother.

Donald Trump signed an executive order to help ensure that religious organizations are not forced to choose between violating their religious beliefs by complying with Obamacare's contraceptive mandate or shutting their doors.

April 20, 2018. The Trump Administration ended the Obama-era policy of listing abortion as a "human right" in the State Department's annual human rights report, and it added a section on population control.

February 22, 2019. The Trump Administration released its final rule for a policy to defund any clinic that either provides abortions or refers people to abortion clinics, something that would reduce Planned Parenthood funding by about $60 million.

Trump signed an order reinstating the Mexico City Policy, which defunded International Planned Parenthood and other organizations that promote foreign abortions. The Organization of American States was the first organization to lose American funding because of the new policy.

April 4, 2017. The Trump Administration halted U.S. funding of the UN Population Fund, which has links to inhumane abortion programs such as China's one-child policy, Instead, the $32.5 million was shifted to the U.S. Agency for International Development.

May 4, 2017. On the annual National Day of Prayer, President Trump signed an executive order on religious liberty. Among its provisions, it loosened IRS restrictions against political activities by tax-exempt religious organizations, effectively weakening the Johnson Amendment; and it attempted to make it easier for employers not to provide contraceptives if they had religious objections. The order gave conservative Attorney General Jeff Sessions greater authority regarding religious liberty policy. Although well-received by some Christians and conservatives, others criticized it for being ineffective and easy to repeal. According to the Family Research Council nearly one year later, the order helped faith-based groups give healthcare coverage to 13.7 million Americans, among other positive effects.

President Trump appointed several pro-life advocates to the Department of Health and Human Services positions. In late March 2017, he appointed Scott Lloyd to lead the HHS's Office of Refugee Resettlement, which led the fight against allowing illegal immigrants obtaining abortions. On April 28, 2017, President Trump appointed Dr. Charmaine Yoest, a strong pro-life advocate and the former president of Americans United for Life, to the position of assistant secretary of public affairs for the Department of Health and Human Services, replacing a strong Planned Parenthood supporter. In late May, Trump appointed Shannon Royce, who formerly served in the Family Research Council and the Southern Baptists' Ethics & Religious Liberty Commission, to the HHS Center for Faith-based and Neighborhood Partnerships. Around May 1, 2017, President Trump appointed Teresa Manning, a pro-life advocate who worked for the Family Research Council and the National Right to Life, to be the HHS deputy assistant secretary for population affairs. In July 2017, President Trump appointed Bethany Kozma, a strong conservative activist who reportedly stated on March 2018 that the U.S. "is a pro-life country" at a private United Nations meeting, as Senior Adviser in the Gender Equality and Women's Empowerment division of USAID. President Trump continued making pro-life political appointments. For example, in June 2018, he appointed Dr. Diane Foley, a pro-life OB/GYN, to run the HHS's family planning program. In November 2018, President Trump appointed Dr. Maureen Condic, a pro-life neurobiologist to the National Science Board.

January 27, 2017. Vice President Mike Pence became the first vice president in United States history to speak at the annual March for Life in Washington D.C. Additionally, Trump senior advisor Kellanne Conway also spoke at the event, and Trump himself strongly expressed his support for the march. Then in January of 2018, President Trump became the first incumbent U.S. president to speak to the March for Life via live video feed, speaking strongly against abortion. He also became the third incumbent president to speak to the rally at all, with the first two, Ronald Reagan and George W. Bush. In 2019 Both President Trump and Vice President Pence made surprise appearances – with Trump speaking through a video feed – at the March for Life, making more strong pro-life statements.

February 5, 2019. In his State of the Union Address, President Trump strongly condemned abortion, stating that "all children — born and unborn — are made in the holy image of God," and he called on Congress to ban late-term abortions.

February 7, 2019. Speaking at the National Prayer Breakfast, President Trump, among other statements, called for "a culture that cherishes dignity and sanctity of innocent human life."

February 14, 2019. President Trump met with several pro-life advocates in the Oval Office, expressing his support for their efforts.

Among other statements defending the sanctity of life, President Trump strongly criticized Democrats for voting against criminalizing infanticide. Other Trump Administration officials spoke against pro-abortion policies, including Vice President Mike Pence and HUD Secretary Ben Carson.

April 2018. When President Trump declared this month National Child Abuse Prevention Month, he included unborn children in his proclamation, stating that "they are endowed from conception with value, purpose, and human dignity."

May 22, 2018. President Trump spoke at the Susan B. Anthony list's annual gala and gave a strong pro-life speech.

The Trump administration proposed new regulations to ensure Title X family planning funding does not go to projects that perform, support or refer patients for abortion. This ensures that taxpayers do not fund the abortion industry in violation of the law and would make sure that grants would also not be used for abortions. Because of the Trump Administration's Title X grant reforms, federal government funding of Planned Parenthood fell significantly in 2019.

On April 23, 2019. Trump successfully got the UN to remove pro-abortion language from a sexual violence resolution.

July 2017. President Trump appointed Bethany Kozma, a conservative homemaker and anti-transgender activist as Senior Adviser in the Gender Equality and Women's Empowerment division of USAID.

March 29, 2019. The Trump Administration announced that for 2019 it would give a $1.7 million grant – money that likely would have originally gone to Planned

Parenthood – to the Obria Group, a crisis pregnancy center which opposes abortion and contraceptives, and it would continue giving grants through 2022.

January 22, 2018. President Trump proclaimed this day National Sanctity of Human Life Day and he did so again in 2019.

February 15, 2019. President Trump commemorated Susan B. Anthony's birthday, noting that "pursuit for equal rights demands respect for all human life, including innocent unborn babies."

Supporting Christian Values As President.
Facts 797-809

August 27, 2018. President Trump hosted a dinner for evangelical Christian leaders, highlighting his support for religious liberty and pro-life policies.

While newly inaugurated U.S. Presidents generally give their first commencement addresses at the University of Notre Dame, President Trump gave his at the conservative Christian Liberty University. One of his lines was, "In America, we don't worship government, we worship God."

It was reported in late April 2017 that nine Trump Administration cabinet members, including Vice President Mike Pence, were participating in a weekly Bible study, and members of the House and Senate were also conducting their own Bible studies. The media took notice of the Bible studies again in late-July 2017. The Bible study was possibly the first one held in the executive branch in at least 100 years. The Trump Administration was described as being "the most evangelical Cabinet in history," and the Bible study suggested that the administration is, at least in part, striving to be under God. In addition to the Bible study, Press Secretary Sarah Huckabee Sanders reads Christian devotionals before each press briefing.

December 11, 2018. President Trump signed the Iraq and Syria Genocide Relief and Accountability Act into law, which ensured that U.S. aid to the Middle East would reach Christians and other religious minorities, and it authorized the government to directly fund faith-based groups and other NGOs working in the region.

January 28, 2019. President Trump endorsed Bible

literacy classes in public schools.

November 23, 2017. President Trump made his Thanksgiving proclamation, stating that "as one people, we seek God's protection, guidance, and wisdom, as we stand humbled by the abundance of our great Nation and the blessings of freedom, family, and faith." Trump mentioned God 8 times in his Thanksgiving address, while Obama did not mention God even once in his 2016 Thanksgiving address.

February 7, 2019. Speaking at the National Prayer Breakfast, President Trump spoke in favor of faith-based adoption organizations and vowed to protect them, among other statements.

By the Trump Administration's second year, conservative and Christian colleges saw more of their students accepted as interns inside the administration than under the entire Obama Administration.

President Trump fought against the War on Christmas in 2017. For Christmas 2017, the White House Christmas card used the term "Merry Christmas," a sharp departure from the Obama Administration, which avoided using the term, instead opting for politically correct alternatives that did not mention "Christmas." The White House also set up a nativity scene with the baby Jesus for Christmas.

January 23, 2019. The Trump Administration announced it would grant a waiver to South Carolina allowing faith-based foster care organizations to still receive funding despite adhering to Christian values on marriage.

July 24–26, 2018. Trump Administration announced the establishment of an International Religious Freedom Fund, as well as the Genocide Recovery and Persecution

Response Program to quickly provide aid to persecuted religious minorities like Christians in other nations.

September 10, 2019. President Trump announced he would lift a federal ban on funding for faith-based historically black colleges and universities.

September 23, 2019. Rather than focus on climate change as most of the UN, President Trump gave a major speech promoting religious freedom, stating that "the United States is founded on the principle that our rights do not come from government they come from God," among other strong statements.

Trump And The Second Amendment.
Facts 810-824

Trump's 2019 ATF (Alcohol Tobacco and Firearms) nominee, Chuck Canterbury, opposes universal background checks and is on record saying "I do believe in the Second Amendment, and I believe that those individual sales are guaranteed under current law."

February 28, 2017. President Trump signed a bill into law repealing a Social Security Administration rule adding mental disability determinations to the background check registry, subject to a person applying to be removed from the list. Congress had passed a law requiring federal agencies to search their records for people who were "mentally defective". The regulation would have added the names of disability beneficiaries who have a mental illness or are not competent to manage their finances, potentially leading to the removal of Second Amendment rights to many perfectly competent, mentally healthy citizens. Trump was able to stop this from going into effect by signing Public Law 115–8.

June 30, 2017. The Trump Administration sent 20 ATF agents to Chicago to help the city fight gun violence. The local US Attorney said the same day that his office had already prosecuted more Chicago gun cases in 2017 than it had done throughout the entire year 2016.

Starting early in his presidency, the Trump Administration undid several Obama-era executive branch gun regulations.

April 21, 2017. President Trump replaced Obama-appointed Vivek Murthy, who was opposed by gun rights groups, as Surgeon General of the United States.

August 16, 2017. The Justice Department terminated Operation Choke Point, a program started during the Obama Administration that existed to encourage banks not to do business with "high risk" businesses and that was criticized by conservatives as unfairly targeting gun dealers and other businesses not looked favorably upon by liberals.

As a sign of confidence in the Trump Administration by Second Amendment supporters, several media outlets reported in 2017 that gun sales fell deeply compared to 2016 when people thought Hillary would be President. It's also interesting to note that background checks have increased to record levels in 2017 even though fewer guns are selling. This is because the number of Americans applying for concealed carry permits have increased. Ultimately, while the number of gun sales in 2017 was significantly lower than in 2016, it is the second-best year on record for gun sales in the U.S.

Trump's bump stock ban was done without signing legislation. The ATF has admitted that it may have exceeded its constitutional power as part of the executive branch in making the ban stating, "The statutory scheme does not, however, appear to provide the Attorney General the authority to engage in 'gap-filling' interpretations of what qualifies as a 'machine-gun.'" In the end, less than 600 of an estimated 500,000 bump stocks were turned into federal authorities.

President Trump became the first president since Ronald Reagan in 1983 to speak at the National Rifle Association's annual convention. He has spoken at the annual convention every year since his election, where he has expressed strong support for Second Amendment rights.

Unlike many politicians, President Trump did not call for gun control immediately after major shootings such as one at a Texas church in November 2017, noting that stronger gun laws would not stop such shootings, the gunman had mental health problems and that it was not "a guns situation," and he noted that the shooter was stopped by another person with a gun.

December 18, 2018. President Trump's commission on school safety released its final report, which among other positive recommendations, called for more armed guards in schools, ending an Obama Administration race-based school discipline policy, and argued against raising the minimum age to buy a gun, rather than calling for more gun control.

March 23, 2018. President Trump signed an omnibus spending bill that Congress sent to him, and its provisions included the Fix-NICS Act, which jeopardized the Second Amendment rights of over 4 million Americans. The omnibus bill also included a clause that clarified that the Center for Disease Control and Prevention could conduct "gun violence research." President Trump signed legislation to improve the Federal firearm background check system and keep guns out of the hands of dangerous criminals.

May 10, 2019. President Trump signed a bill into law that gave states an increased ability to build or expand public shooting ranges.

April 26, 2019. President Trump announced the U.S. would withdraw the U.S. signature from the United Nations Arms Trade Treaty, which former President Obama signed in 2013 and which threatened Second

Amendment rights. President Trump signed a letter to the U.S. Senate asking it to stop the process of ratifying the treaty. In announcing the decision, President Trump stated that "under my administration, we will never surrender American sovereignty to anyone" and that "we will never allow foreign bureaucrats to trample on your Second Amendment freedom."

August 1, 2019. President Trump commemorated National Shooting Sports Month, stating that "the vibrant shooting sports culture is made possible, in large part, by our steadfast protection of one of our bedrock and most-cherished liberties, the right to keep and bear arms."

Concerning The Environment And Climate Change.
Facts 825-850

December 8, 2016. President-elect Trump nominated Oklahoma Attorney General Scott Pruitt, a conservative and a critic of the Environmental Protection Agency, as its head. The U.S. Senate confirmed Pruitt on February 17, 2017. By his first year in office, Scott Pruitt sharply reoriented the EPA in a strongly conservative direction, having it focus on "protecting the nation's air, water, and public health" rather than advance left-wing environmentalist goals. While continuing to consult with environmental organizations, Pruitt also met with business organizations, and the EPA re-established a program to formally work with industries when making regulations.

August 2017. The Trump Administration named Cathy Stepp, a conservative skeptic on human-caused climate change, to lead the EPA Midwest regional office. The EPA then appointed a former Trump campaign aide to make the decisions regarding grant funding.

By the end of 2017, the Trump Administration had taken numerous steps to undo the Obama Administration's environmental policies and regulations. The shift in the Trump Administration regarding energy and the environment was illustrated with the replacement of a page about climate change on the official White House website with one about the "America First Energy Plan."

Because of Trump, changes were made to the Environmental Protection Agency website including the organization's dismissal of global warmist scientific advisers from the EPA and Interior Department to replace them with individuals who better understand the effects of regulations.

February 28, 2017. President Trump signed an executive order directing the EPA to start the process of repealing the Obama Administration's Waters of the United States rule. The "Waters of the United States" rule (WOTUS) grants the EPA jurisdiction over even the smallest bodies of water, whether anyone is trying to get clean drinking water from it or not. It's a vast expansion of jurisdiction over the Clean Water Rule which puts farmers and industry at odds with environmentalists. The rule gave Washington, DC bureaucrats unprecedented powers to regulate virtually any place that water flows or accumulates anywhere in the United States. It allowed regulation of a host of land features, including minor wetlands and typically dry stream-beds that only occasionally carry storm-water. The Clean Water Act says that the EPA can regulate 'navigable waters,' meaning waters that truly affect interstate commerce. But a few years ago, the EPA decided that 'navigable waters' can mean nearly every puddle or every ditch on a farmer's land, or anyplace else that they decide. The EPA under Trump began the process of repealing WOTUS on June 27, 2017 and was formally repealed September 12, 2019.

On March 18, 2017 the Trump administration forced the G-20 to remove any mention of climate change from its joint statement. The G-20 is a group of twenty finance ministers and central bank governors in an international forum that promotes discussion and offers policy suggestions among the nations having the 20 largest economies, supposedly intending to promote global economic stability and growth.

May 2017. The Trump Administration signed agreements as a member of the Arctic Council, and it was later revealed that it successfully weakened the language regarding climate change and environmental policy.

June 1, 2017. To the dismay of world leaders, the media, liberals, and in a major blow to Obama's legacy, President Trump announced the U.S. would withdraw from the Paris Climate Agreement and immediately stop its implementation, including by ending payments to the U.N. Green Climate Fund. In his announcement speech, Trump made clear "I was elected to represent the citizens of Pittsburgh, not Paris," and that "our withdrawal from the agreement represents a reassertion of America's sovereignty." Despite leaving the agreement, the U.S. saw the largest drop in carbon emissions of any country in 2017 even as the global level of emissions rose, and the EPA reported that U.S. emissions dropped 2.7%, a greater decrease than in 2016.

August 15, 2017. President Trump signed an executive order to speed up environmental reviews for infrastructure project approvals.

August 20, 2017. The Trump Administration did not renew the charter for the federal advisory panel for climate change, disbanding the group.

December 18, 2017. Among the many other aspects of President Trump's national security strategy, the Trump Administration reversed the Obama administration's decision to list climate change as a national security threat and even suggested that the climate change lobby is a national security threat.

March 23, 2018. While opposing much of President Trump's conservative environmental agenda, Congress did allow the Trump Administration to end NASA's Carbon Monitoring System, a program to measure world carbon emissions and associated with the Paris Agreement.

March 23, 2018. President Trump signed a bill to reduce the regulatory burden on farmers by exempting them from having to report emissions from animal waste, something the EPA implemented on July 23, 2018.

April 12, 2018. President Trump signed a memorandum ordering the EPA to take several steps to make it easier for states and companies to comply with air pollution regulations, such as having the EPA speed up its decision making on granting air pollution permits. It was reported shortly afterward that the EPA had issued several other memos in the previous months rolling back several air pollution regulations.

April 24, 2018. Trump's EPA Administrator Scott Pruitt signed an order to create a rule requiring any scientific study used to justify additional regulations to be made public, thus eliminating "secret science."

May 17, 2018. President Trump signed an executive order requiring federal agencies to reduce waste and the amount of energy they use, among other measures to promote environmental and energy efficiency. This order replaced a stricter and less flexible order signed by Obama in 2015.

June 19, 2018. President Trump signed an executive order on U.S. management of ocean resources that replaced a policy enacted by Obama in 2010 by reducing bureaucracy and encouraging offshore development.

July 19, 2018. The Trump Administration announced it would change how it enforces the Endangered Species Act, streamlining its enforcement and reducing the regulatory burden on Americans, among other changes.

The Trump Administration took a conservative, commonsense approach when dealing with the major wildfires in California in 2018. For example, the U.S. Forest Service moved to expand logging in the Los Padres National Forest to reduce the risk of forest fires, and on August 8, 2018, the Commerce Department ordered the National Marines Fisheries Service to prioritize water for fighting fires over protecting endangered species. These actions came roughly when President Trump criticized California's environmental laws for making the wildfires in the state so much worse, and Interior Secretary Ryan Zinke also strongly criticized environmentalists and called for forest management.

On December 22, 2018. President Trump signed an executive order directing the Interior and Agriculture departments to develop a plan to better manage the forests on federal land after the terrible wildfires in CA.

October 8, 2018. Fulfilling a campaign promise, the Trump Administration announced a higher percentage of ethanol to be sold in gasoline year-round, relaxing federal regulations. The EPA moved the implement the order in March 2019.

Trump warned San Francisco that he'd hit them with EPA violations unless they could get control over all of the waste on the streets that are left there by the homeless population. "They have to clean it up. We can't have our cities going to hell," Trump said. Some of that wastes find it's way into storm drains and from there the ocean.

October 19, 2018. President Trump signed a memorandum to reduce regulations on water supply so western states could receive more water.

Trump wanted the EPA to host debates on the existence and nature of climate change but White House Chief of

Staff John F. Kelly wouldn't allow it.

February 20, 2019. The Trump Administration announced it would reduce grazing fees for federal land.

President Trump skipped the U.N. Climate Summit in 2019.

Trump On Border Security.
Facts 851-875

Simply because of Trump's rhetoric by his 100th day in office, borders crossings were reported to have fallen by 73%.

President Trump secured $1.6 billion for border wall construction in the March 2018 omnibus bill.

February 15, 2019. Trump declared a national emergency to allocate funds to build a wall on the border with Mexico. During the announcement, the president says he expects the declaration to be challenged in court, which it was. According to the White House, up to $8.1 billion will become available to build the border wall including: $601 million from the Treasury Forfeiture Fund, up to $2.5 billion under the Department of Defense funds transferred for Support for Counter-drug Activities, up to $3.6 billion reallocation from the Department of Defense military construction projects, and the $1.375 billion from a congressional spending package.

Although the declaration received criticism from congressional Democrats for his national emergency for border wall funds—even before the official announcement — since 1976, American presidents have declared nearly 60 national emergencies. That's an average of 1.333 declarations per president.

Since Trump took office not a single cage has been constructed to hold migrants. All those cages seen on the news were constructed by President Obama's administration and previous administrations. "I've been to that facility, where they talk about cages. That facility was built under President Obama under (Homeland Security) Secretary Jeh Johnson. I was there because I was there when it was built," said Thomas Homan, who was Obama's executive associate director of Immigration and Customs Enforcement for nearly four years.

May 30, 2019. Trump threatened to impose new tariffs on Mexico if the country did not step up its immigration enforcement actions, saying in a White House statement that a round of tariffs would begin on June 10 at 5% "on all goods imported from Mexico." The statement warned further that if Mexico does not act as Trump's demands, tariffs would continue to increase up to a permanent level of 25% by October. June 7, 2019, Trump says tariffs on Mexican goods are "indefinitely suspended" after negotiators from the US and Mexico were able to reach a deal on immigration enforcement. According to the Washington Post, the number of family-unit apprehensions on the southern border has declined about 13 percent since the start of June that year. The decline is partly attributed to action taken by Mexico to more strictly enforce its border to avoid the possible imposition of tariffs.

President Trump labeled Democrats "border deniers" for their pro-open borders policies.

Trump gave the Democrats the option of allowing illegal immigrants into sanctuary cities in exchange for funding for the Border Wall, and they refused.

In August 2019 border patrol unveiled 60 new miles of border wall built in Arizona and expected another 450 miles to be built by the end of 2020.

Illegal immigration declined dramatically after Trump took office. According to data released early in Trump's presidency, illegal border crossings decreased by 40% in the first month a remarkable achievement, considering that illegal immigration usually increases by 10 to 20% in January and February.

Under Trump, Customs and Border Protection apprehended 17,256 criminals and 1,019 gang members in 2018. ICE's Enforcement and Removal Operations arrested 158,581 aliens in 2018, an 11 percent increase from 2017. Ninety percent of those arrested had criminal convictions, pending charges, or had been issued final orders of removal. CE ERO increased removals by 13 percent in 2018 to 256,086, the majority of whom were convicted criminals. Removals of convicted criminal aliens increased by 14 percent from 2017. Nearly 6,000 known or suspected gang members were removed in 2018, a 9 percent increase from 2017. The Department of Justice prosecuted a record number of criminal immigration offenses in 2018 and increased the number of prosecutions for illegal entry by 84 percent over 2017.

Trump getting Mexico to aid in stopping illegals from entering the United States is credited in helping reduce the number of people apprehended by 22% in 2019. Trump reaffirms that the numbers are still at a crisis level and more work is needed to be done.

Trump has convinced the Salvadoran government to deploy hundreds of police, soldiers, and agents totaling over a thousand to its border with Guatemala to aid in preventing future illegal aliens from making it to the US.

Because of Trump's policies the DHS's Office of Immigration Statistics, illegally entering the U.S. from Mexico was harder than it had ever been in decades, at least, and smuggling costs doubled from the late 2000s.

H.R. 244, which was signed into law by President Trump on May 5, 2017, and funded the government through September 30, 2017, did not include funding for several of President Trump's priorities, such as defunding sanctuary cities and building new sections of the border wall. However, it did include an additional $1.5 billion in border security funding, including money to repair 40 miles of existing border barrier sections and to increase funding for ICE and CBP, among other conservative achievements.

July 17, 2017. The Trump Administration, in a break with the Obama Administration's refusal to do likewise, gave $2.3 million to the state of Texas so its military patrol could continue patrolling the border with Mexico.

March 23, 2018. Despite doing significantly less to advance his conservative immigration agenda than he hoped, the omnibus bill that President Trump signed did spend nearly $1.6 billion on border security, including money for building new sections of the border barrier, repairing existing sections, and building secondary fencing.

April 4, 2018. President Trump signed an order deploying National Guard soldiers to secure the border and assist border patrol agents. The Department of Defense quickly took steps to deploy National Guard troops, and Secretary of Defense James Mattis signed an order on April 6, 2018, to approve funding for up to 4,000 troops. By May 9,

2018, the CBP announced that because of the National Guard troops it had apprehended 1,600 additional illegals and turned back an additional 451.

October 26, 2018. Directed by Trump, Defense Secretary Mattis approved a request from the DHS to send an unspecified number of active-duty soldiers to the border with Mexico to help U.S. Border Patrol, something done as a large migrant caravan approached the U.S. On October 29, 2018, the Pentagon announced it would initially deploy about 5,200 troops to the border, and U.S. troops began deployment shortly afterward. The soldiers immediately went to work securing the border and put up several miles of razor wire on existing border barriers. On December 4, 2018, Defense Secretary Mattis approved a DHS request to extend troop employment until January 31, 2019, from the original end date of December 15, 2018.

Among other border security improvements, the Trump administration constructed 20 miles of new and improved fencing in New Mexico. The DHS also constructed 2.25 miles of improved fencing and border infrastructure at Calexico, California, as well as 14 miles in San Diego. The Rio Grande Valley also saw improved border security measures, and the DHS waived environmental regulations in 2018 to expedite the construction of about 17 miles of wall in the area. In September 2018, the CBP began construction of an improved four-mile border barrier in El Paso. The CBP also began preparations for a six-mile border wall construction project in Texas scheduled to begin in February 2019, an eight-mile construction project in Texas scheduled to begin at the same time, and a 32-mile wall replacement project in Arizona to start in April 2019. February 2019, the DHS waived several environmental laws to allow it to build several miles of wall in San Diego, and construction began later that month. In

April 2019, the CBP began construction of 13 miles of wall in Texas. On April 27, 2019, the DHS waived environmental laws to speed up the building of 53 miles of wall in Arizona and Texas, and on May 14, 2019, it again waived environmental laws to speed up border wall construction in California and Arizona. In May 2019, Customs and Border Protection approved a $42.8 million contract to build three miles of border wall in Starr County, Texas. On June 27, 2019, the federal government announced a contract to build four miles of border wall in Texas.

July 1, 2019. President Trump signed a $4.6 billion humanitarian border spending bill. Democrat House Speaker Nancy Pelosi failed to pass a partisan left-wing bill and caved into passing a bipartisan Senate bill, though the Senate bill also included some liberal provisions.

March 15, 2019. President Trump signed an executive order that updated a 2011 order signed by President Obama, strengthening the definition of a "significant transnational criminal organization" so that the Trump Administration could better counter Mexican cartels and other similar organizations.

May 8, 2019. The Trump administration moved to implement a program to allow Border Patrol agents to act as asylum officers to help reduce mass migration and speech up asylum claim processing.

In a Trump victory, the Supreme Court ruled in his favor when they struck down a block which will now allow Trump to appropriate military funding to build the border wall.

The Huffington Post released an article originally titled "The Dreadful Truth: Trump Got His Wall." In it, they claim

Trump has constructed "zero" miles of physical barrier along the southern border but has stopped immigration another way. They talk about how through the cumulative of subtle administrative shifts they call Trump's "invisible wall." The evidence they use to explain is that in the two years Trump has been president, denials for H1B visas have doubled, wait times have doubled, and the average processing times have increased 46% even as the number of applicants has gone down. Also, the number of immigrants added to the U.S. in 2018 was 70% lower than it was in 2016.

Immigration.
Facts 876-916

President Trump released an immigration framework that would fix the broken immigration system through merit-based reform and provide the resources needed to secure the border. This includes closing the legal loopholes that enable illegal immigration, ending chain migration, and eliminating the visa lottery.

Trump set the refugee cap for 2019 at 30,000. This is a significant reduction from 45,000 in 2018 and President Obama's cap for 2017 of 110,000.

It was reported in July 2017 that due to President Trump's strong immigration enforcement policies, numerous illegal immigrants chose to self-deport rather than being prosecuted and deported. In addition, many illegal immigrants fearing deportation fled to Canada, a trend that continued after the end of 2017. The number of migrants coming into Canada became so large that the Canadian government sent soldiers to take care of the situation. The surge in illegal immigration to Canada that was attributed to President Trump and his policies continued into 2018, and Canada's Immigration and Refugee Board was "overwhelmed" by the number of migrants entering the country. On July 18, 2018, Prime Minister Justin Trudeau even appointed a minister in charge of border security to combat the problem.

Trump signed Executive Order 13780, titled "Protecting the Nation from Foreign Terrorist Entry into the United States," ensured that foreign nationals were properly vetted before they gain entry to the country. This EO revised and replaced the similar order the President signed in January. The revised executive order imposed a temporary freeze on entry by individuals from six countries that are hotbeds for terrorism, and suspended the entry into the U.S. for 90 days for aliens from the following countries: Iran, Syria, Libya, Somalia, Yemen, and Sudan.

Trump signed Executive Order 13768, titled "Enhancing Public Safety in the Interior of the United States," stated that sanctuary jurisdictions who refused to comply with immigration enforcement measures would not be eligible to receive Federal grants, except as deemed necessary for law enforcement purposes by the Attorney General or Secretary of Homeland Security.

November 2018 President Trump signed a presidential proclamation to make alterations to the asylum process by attempting to reduce the flood of migrants who enter the United States illegally before asking for asylum. Under an interim final rule that implements the proclamation, individuals wishing to file an asylum claim will be required to present themselves at legal ports of entry, where a determination can be made about whether they have a 'credible fear' of persecution in their homelands. Those with valid credible fear claims will be admitted to the United States. FAIR President Dan Stein hailed the proclamation as a "necessary first step" in protecting the integrity of our asylum laws.

The Trump Administration published its proposed rule on public charge exclusions— reiterating the common-sense notion that no immigrant should become a burden to the United States. Immigrants are supposed to be a benefit, not a hardship, to the United States. Additionally, welfare programs are meant to serve the most vulnerable of Americans as stopgap measures to assist them during their times of need. This proposed rule remains in line with President Trump's campaign promise to put Americans first.

It was reported that Trump was considering renaming the largest migrant detention center to "The Barack Hussein Obama II Detention Center."

Efforts have been made by journalists to paint Trump as advocating for a Muslim registry, but what he proposed was a database for Syrian refugees.

The Administration has more than doubled the number of jurisdictions participating in the 287(g) program, which enables State and local law enforcement to aid immigration enforcement.

January 27, 2017. Right after taking office Trump signed an executive order indefinitely banning the admission of Syrian refugees and suspended the overall refugee program for 120 days. By 2018 Trump reduced refugee admissions 75% compared to Obama in 2016.

President Trump signed an executive order regarding the temporary suspension of refugees and others from certain high-risk countries after the first one was blocked by the courts. A second order he signed in March made some clarifications and minor improvements over the first, such as exempting green card holders from the ban and excluding Iraq from it as it had developed an acceptable vetting process.

Trump made it clear that he would help Christian refugees, a reversal from the Obama Administration and by the end of 2017 Christian refugees comprised 53.2% of those admitted into the U.S., versus 32% Muslims, with the numbers flipping from the previous year. By contrast, Trump admitted as many refugees in 2017 as Obama did in his last three months in office.

By 2019, Christian refugees increased to 80% of the refugees admitted by Trump.

In late March/early April 2017, the Trump Administration cracked down on H-1B visas in a series of actions, making it much more difficult for entry-level programmers to enter the U.S, combating corruption in the program, and making sure that Americans were not discriminated against. On April 18, 2017, President Trump signed an executive order restricting the H-1B visa to give hiring preference to American workers and enacting stronger enforcement of laws requiring the use of American-made materials in federal projects. Experts on the H-1B visa supported his order.

July 2017. The Trump administration changed the focus of Citizenship and Immigration Services from "integration," as it was under the Obama Administration, to "assimilation." This could be seen in the renaming of a grant program that started under the Obama administration from the "Citizenship and Integration Grant Program" to the "Citizenship and Assimilation Grant Program."

September 24, 2017. The Trump administration established a new travel ban that affected 8 countries – Chad, Iran, Libya, North Korea, Somalia, Syria, Yemen, and certain individuals from Venezuela. According to the U.S. government, these countries fell under the travel ban due to not sharing information about terrorism and the people applying to the U.S. In December 2017, the Supreme Court allowed the Trump Administration to fully enforce the travel ban despite left-wing opposition, and the State Department began fully implementing it a few days later. On April 10, 2018, President Trump signed an order to remove Chad from the list. On June 26, 2018, the Supreme Court issued a final ruling in favor of the travel ban, in a major victory for the administration.

April 22, 2019. President Trump signed a memorandum ordering his administration to find ways to reduce visa overstay rates.

July 2, 2019. The Trump Administration began efforts to impose fines on illegal aliens who disobeyed deportation orders and remained in the U.S.

July 22, 2019. The Trump Administration announced it would fully enforce a 1996 law by implementing a policy of quickly deporting, without a trial, illegals in the U.S. for less than two years.

September 29, 2017. President Trump signed an order to allow up to only 45,000 refugees into the country in 2018, the lowest cap since the Refugee Act of 1980 was signed and a 59% decrease compared to the cap that President Obama had proposed for 2017.

December 2, 2017. The Trump administration pulled out of the Global Compact on Migration a United Nations agreement, due to its infringing on U.S. sovereignty and its immigration policies. U.S. Ambassador Nikki Haley stated that "our decisions on immigration policies must always be made by Americans and Americans alone," and that "the global approach in the New York Declaration is simply not compatible with U.S. sovereignty."

President Trump signed a memorandum that will finally enforce a 23-year-old provision requiring sponsors of legal immigrants to reimburse the government for any social services the immigrant uses in the United States. The provision was part of a welfare reform package signed into law in 1996 by then-President Bill Clinton, but which has not been consistently enforced until now. Under the provision and President Trump's memorandum, future immigrant sponsors will be required to sign an affidavit ensuring financial responsibility for the sponsored immigrant. Additionally, the memo creates a collection mechanism to recover any needed funds from the sponsor.

President Trump issued a Presidential Memorandum directing his administration to curb the ongoing asylum abuse occurring at our borders. In the Presidential Memo, the President directed his administration to propose regulations that would: streamline court proceedings for aliens who pass initial credible fear determinations; adjudicate all asylum applications in immigration courts within 180 days of filing; require fees for asylum applications and work permit applications; bar aliens who have entered (or attempted to enter) the country illegally from receiving provisional work permits prior to being approved for relief; and immediately revoke the work authorization of aliens who receive final removal orders.

December 15, 2017. The Trump administration added new requirements for countries participating in the U.S. Visa Waiver Program to help vet travelers entering the U.S. and to prevent visa overstays in the U.S.

In 2017, the Trump administration announced it would end "Temporary Protected Status" for Sudan, Nicaragua, and Haiti. The State Department also reportedly paved the way for the U.S. government to revoke additional TPS protections in 2018.

Late May 2017. The State Department introduced new and much stricter rules for vetting all people seeking a visa to enter the U.S., with the introduction of social media vetting being among the changes. Trump moved to make these measures permanent on August 3, 2017.

June 21, 2017. President Trump signed an executive order, rescinding a guideline signed by former President Obama to speed up vetting times for people seeking visas, to improve vetting standards.

August 2017. The Trump Administration continued strengthening the vetting of immigrants, such as requiring some to prove their ability to return to their home countries if necessary, to crack down on visa overstays, and requiring some of those seeking green cards to conduct an in-person interview.

It was reported that the Trump Administration, due to the president's previous executive orders, had ended Obama's "home free magnet" policy, where illegal immigrants who did not commit a serious crime (other than crossing the border illegally) did not need to fear deportation because ICE needed to gain permission from the Field Office Director before deporting them; and the Trump Administration expanded the use of expedited removal proceedings, thus, illegal immigrants "without violent criminal histories" could be arrested and deported.

By the beginning of 2019, the Trump Administration was able to reduce the number of countries "that habitually refuse to take back immigrants whom the U.S. is trying to deport" from 23 to 9. He did this by enacting visa sanctions on countries that continued to refuse to accept deportees until they changed their policy. Also, the number of "at-risk" countries fell from 62 to 24.

It was reported in June 2017 that the Trump Administration began repatriating illegal immigrants given "administrative closure" by the Obama Administration, a form of "quasi-amnesty." Due to this change in policy, as it was reported a month later on July 2017, the number of deportation cases in Los Angeles alone rose 60%.

June 2017. The Trump Administration ended the Family Case Management Program, which allowed certain illegal immigrants seeking asylum to stay out of detention centers.

President Trump has appointed several strong conservatives to positions where they can have an impact on immigration enforcement. He appointed Thomas Homan, someone with a reputation for enforcing immigration laws, as acting director of Immigration and Customs Enforcement. On January 31, President Trump appointed Ronald Vitiello, who was endorsed by the National Border Patrol Council to lead U.S. Border Patrol. In late March 2017, President Trump appointed Scott Lloyd, a strong conservative supportive of the president's immigration policies, to lead the HHS's Office of Refugee Resettlement. President Trump appointed two conservatives on immigration issues to senior positions in the Department of Homeland Security. March 2018— President Trump appointed Andrew Veprek, a White House aide described as having strong pro-American immigration views, as a deputy assistant secretary at the Bureau of Population, Refugees and Migration. July 2018, President Trump appointed John Zadrozny, a White

House aid opposed to mass migration, to serve on the State Department's Policy Planning Staff where he would influence matters related to the department's migration policies. The USCIS worked to implement President Trump's agenda, and in June 2019, the president appointed Ken Cuccinelli, a strong conservative, to lead the agency.

November 13, 2018. The U.S. voted against a UN General Assembly resolution praising the UNHCR and endorsing the Global Compact for Refugees – the latter of which the U.S. announced it would withdraw from – because it conflicted with American "sovereign interests." That resolution had previously been approved by consensus in the 60 years of its existence before the Trump administration requested a vote on the matter, and the U.S. was the only country to vote against the resolution. The Trump Administration continued its opposition to the globalist Global Compact on Migration in 2018, voting against it during UN votes on December 10, 17 and 19. Numerous other countries began following the Trump Administration's lead in opposing the migration compact.

June 20, 2018. While President Trump caved to the Left and the mainstream media by signing an executive order to prevent the separation of illegal migrant families while being detained, the order kept the administration's "zero-tolerance" enforcement policy in place, and it directed the Justice Department to challenge a 2015 court settlement that required the federal government to release illegal migrants with children. In a court filing on June 29, 2018, the DOJ announced a new policy where it would seek to detain illegal migrant families indefinitely, and on September 6, 2018, the DHS and HHS proposed a rule to allow them to detain illegal migrant families long-term.

March 26, 2018. The Commerce Department announced it would re-add a question to the U.S. Census asking U.S. residents if they are U.S. citizens.

July 11, 2019. President Trump signed an executive order directing the federal government to estimate the number of U.S. citizens through existing government records.

May 23, 2019. President Trump signed a memorandum directing his administration to enforce a provision found in two laws enacted in 1996 requiring the sponsors of legal immigrants to reimburse the government for any welfare benefits used by those immigrants. In June 2019, USCIS announced it had begun implementing the memo. On August 12, 2019, the Trump Administration issued the finalized rule implementing the policy.

February 7, 2019. President Trump signed a proclamation extending a previous order signed in November 2018 that banned migrants illegally entering the U.S. from applying for asylum. On May 8, 2019, President Trump again extended the order through a proclamation.

By 2019, President Trump's 2017 travel ban had ended nearly all immigration from the eight impacted countries.

Random Trump Facts.
Facts 917-970

The President implemented a five-year ban on lobbying for White House employees and a lifetime ban on lobbying for foreign countries.

Trump recognized Jerusalem as the capital of Israel as he promised.

At a summit in 2019 called the Christ Church Call to Action, France, Germany, Britain, and New Zealand demanded that social media companies clamp down on extremism. President Trump publicly refused to co-sign the call for action. Trump was heavily criticized for this but he couldn't legally sign it. The First Amendment wouldn't now allow the President to sign an international agreement that would science the speech of U.S. citizens and the Supreme Court has ruled that the government can't restrict access to social media.

September 3, 2017. President Trump declared that day a National Day of Prayer for victims of Hurricane Harvey, which had just caused devastation in Texas and Louisiana.

Barack Obama believes Donald Trump raised the birth certificate issue because of his skin color and his father's Islamic faith but Bill O'Reilly who knew Trump well thinks differently. He believes Trump planned to galvanize political support among Americans who disliked President Obama, to demonize him in a personal way. Trump established himself as an anti-Obama person and that resonated well with a lot of Americans.

Trump released an America first National Security Strategy.

Cent Uygur of the Young Turks said if Trump avoids war with Iran he will be a better president than George W Bush.

Several news outlets reported that the CIA had to remove a top spy from Russia over the fear that the person could be compromised by Trump. A day later the story was proven to be fake news as the CIA came out and slammed outlets like CNN. The news outlets all redacted the story the next day.

When Trump hired Sarah Sanders as White House Press Secretary he was hiring only the third woman and the first mother to the job.

Trump helped win the U.S. bid for the 2028 Summer Olympics in Los Angeles.

Trump helped win U.S.-Mexico-Canada's united bid for the 2026 World Cup.

Trump signs Executive Order 13799 titled, "the Establishment of Presidential Advisory Commission on Election Integrity," established the Commission on Election Integrity, which reviews claims of voter fraud and improper registration. The commission was ultimately disbanded by President Trump on January 2018. "Despite substantial evidence of voter fraud, many states have refused to provide the [Presidential Advisory Commission on Election Integrity] with basic information relevant to its inquiry," stated the White House. The investigation itself was transferred to the DHS.

Trump had a 95-year-old former Nazi collaborator, who served as a labor camp guard during World War II deported to Germany after a long immigration battle in the United States. Palij, a former concentration camp guard, immigrated to the United States in 1949 and became a citizen in 1957. At the time, he lied to U.S. immigration officials about his role in the war. It was not until much later that federal authorities learned of Palij's true involvement as a guard, and his citizenship was revoked in 2003. The United States cannot criminally prosecute World War II crimes that were carried out overseas, but Palij's deportation was ordered in 2004 after a judge said he had falsified his immigration application. Despite his deportation order, Palij remained in the United States for more than a decade because no other nation was willing to take him.

September 7, 2018. The Interior Department under Trump's guidance finalized a rule to allow new or expanded hunting or fishing on 30 wildlife refuges.

March 12, 2019. In a major public lands and conservation bill that President Trump into law, millions of acres of public land were open to hunters by removing restrictions and made it harder for the government to close off such lands to hunting.

June 5, 2019. The Interior Department announced it would allow hunting and fishing on an additional 1.4 million acres of federal land, a major expansion and something accomplished by Trump eliminating 7,500 regulations.

April 26, 2017. President Trump signed an executive order

ordering Secretary of Education Betsy DeVos to review the Department of Education regulations, to return power to the states and local governments.

January 22–28, 2017. Trump proclaimed is week National School Choice Week, he did again in 2018 and 2019.

March 21, 2019. President Trump signed an executive order to protect campus free speech rights by denying federal research funding to universities that do not protect free speech.

April 9, 2019. It was reported that the Trump Administration had required Texas Tech University's medical school to stop using race as a factor in its admissions policy.

March 21, 2017. President Trump signed a bill into law not only funding NASA but setting a goal of having humans visit Mars "in the 2030s" and potentially colonizing another planet. The bill also funded the agency, the first time such a bill was signed into law in seven years.

June 30, 2017. President Trump signed an executive order re-establishing the National Space Council.

June 18, 2018. President Trump signed a directive ordering the Defense and Commerce Departments to improve their ability to track space junk and to limit the amount of it.

December 11, 2017. President Trump signed a policy directive ordering NASA to "refocus America's space program on human exploration and discovery" and send astronauts back to the Moon and eventually to Mars.

May 5, 2017. President Trump attached a signing statement to a five-month spending bill he signed, ignoring several liberal provisions, such as a statement ordering the administration not to enforce federal marijuana laws in states with medical marijuana.

October 25, 2018. President Trump signed a memorandum reversing two Obama-era memos and ordering the Department of Commerce to develop a national spectrum strategy to speed up the implementation of 5G networks.

May 1, 2017. President Trump proclaimed that day as Loyalty Day, to "recognize and reaffirm our allegiance" to American values, such as "individual liberties, to limited government, and the inherent dignity of every human being."

February 9, 2018. President Trump signed a government funding bill that also had a provision assuring disaster relief from FEMA to churches and other houses of worship and ending the agency's practice of denying funds to the institutions simply because of their religious status.

November 7, 2017. President Trump commemorated the National Day for the Victims of Communism.

June 18, 2017. In celebrating Father's Day, President Trump stated that "fathers have the ability and responsibility to instill in us core values we carry into adulthood. The examples they set and the lessons they impart about hard work, dedication to family, faith in God, and believing in ourselves establish the moral foundation

for success that allows us to live up to our full potential."
The Department of Education invited members of the
Family Research Council and Focus on the Family to a
Father's Day event.

October 13, 2017. President Donald Trump became the
first sitting U.S. President to speak at the Family
Research Council's Value Voters Summit, in which he
voiced strong support for socially conservative policies.

November 19–25, 2017. President Trump declared this
week to be National Family Week to "emphasize the
importance of preserving and promoting strong families,
the cornerstone of our society."

President Trump denounced socialism several times in
2019. In his State of the Union Address on February 5,
2019, President Trump condemned socialism, stating that
"America was founded on liberty and independence and
not government coercion, domination, and control" and
that "we renew our resolve that America will never be a
socialist country." On February 18, 2019, in a speech
primarily condemning Venezuela's Maduro regime,
President Trump strongly denounced socialism. Among
other Trump Administration officials, Larry Kidlow strongly
condemned socialism at CPAC, along with Vice President
Mike Pence. Council of Economic Advisers chairman
Kevin Hassett also criticized socialism. In a March 2019
interview, President Trump described socialism as
"seductive" and "tough to govern on, because the country
goes down the tubes." On March 19, 2019, speaking with
conservative Brazilian President Jair Bolsonaro, President
Trump again criticized socialism, and at another meeting
with Bolsonaro on June 28, 2019, Trump again criticized
socialism and joked that the Democratic Party would
rename itself the "Socialist Party." On July 15, 2019,
President Trump again criticized the Democratic Party for

its embracing of socialism.

March 27, 2019. President Trump signed a memorandum directing his administration to develop a plan to reform the federal housing-finance system.

According to an October 2017 report, Trump attacked the media more than anything else on Twitter.

According to White House Transition Project director Martha Joynt Kumar, by late April 2018, President Trump had answered questions from the media more frequently than Obama had by the same point in his presidency.

January 17, 2018. President Trump released his "2017 Fake News Awards", which was awarded to mainstream media outlets for false stories related to himself. There were eleven winners, with *The New York Times* in first place and with *CNN* in the list four times.

January 21–22, 2019. President Trump strongly criticized the media's handling of an incident involving Catholic students wearing MAGA hats who were falsely accused of harassing an American Indian activist, describing it as a symbol "of Fake News and how evil it can be."

May 15, 2019. The Trump Administration refused to join an international agreement intended to fight "online extremism," with the administration citing its support for free speech as a reason as well as its concern that the agreement would contradict First Amendment rights.

According to the analytics firm CrowdTangle, President Trump's Twitter account received the most interaction of any account on the social media platform.

In August 2017, after violent and deadly clashes between

white supremacists and Antifa activists in Charlottesville, Virginia, President Trump not only strongly criticized the hatred and violence, but, challenging the politically correct attitude of the establishment and the Left, criticized the "many sides" that were responsible for the hatred and violence rather than just the white supremacists. Trump urged all Americans to view themselves as Americans first, saying that "above all, we must remember this truth, no matter our color, creed, religion or political party, we are all Americans first." President Trump stood unmoved even after intense media criticism, and in a press conference held a few days later, he again stated that the alt-left was just as responsible for the violence as the alt-right, criticized the media for its one-sidedness and double standards in reporting on the violence, and criticized the Left's opposition to Confederate monuments.

President Trump signed a Senate Resolution condemning white supremacism and neo-Nazis, he again condemned "hatred, bigotry, and racism in all forms" and said through a White House statement that "no matter the color of our skin or our ethnic heritage, we all live under the same laws, we all salute the same great flag, and we are all made by the same almighty God."

On August 11, 2018, commemorating the one-year anniversary of the Charlottesville violence, President Trump again condemned "all types of racism and acts of violence" and wished "peace to ALL Americans."

On April 26, 2019, President Trump strongly defended comments he made about Robert E. Lee and referred to him as "a great general."

President Trump voiced support for letting Confederate monuments stay, as opposed to taking them down as supported by the Left. He also opposed taking down other statues opposed by leftists, such as those of Christopher Columbus.

May 26, 2017. President Trump did not hold a Ramadan dinner, breaking the annual tradition held since Bill Clinton's presidency. The next year when hosting his first Ramadan dinner, President Trump disinvited Muslim organizations tied to the Muslim Brotherhood, something in contrast to Obama when he hosted the dinners.

President Trump took a strong stance in advocating that NFL players be required to stand for the U.S. National Anthem, and in criticizing the fact that many of them chose to kneel for the anthem. In May 2018, the NFL decided to require its players and other personnel to stand for the anthem.

In August 2018, after ESPN stopped airing the National Anthem, President Trump started a petition calling on ESPN to air the playing of the National Anthem.

President Trump did not proclaim June 2017 as LGBT Pride Month, unlike former presidents Clinton and Obama.

Loves gangster films like Goodfellas, The Godfather Part 1 and 2.

On October 9, 2017. President Trump commemorated Columbus Day without criticizing the holiday as Obama had done despite growing opposition to the holiday from left-wing individuals. Trump made similar statements in 2018 and 2019.

When there was a proposed construction of a mosque near Ground Zero in NYC it was a very sensitive topic. Trump stepped in and tried to find a reasonable solution, he tried to buy the site and offered to locate the mosque in a more appropriate area. The media attacked him for this.

Donald Trump acknowledged John McCain's heroism four times before making the "I like people who weren't captured" comment, but the media chooses to only remember the latter. And after that comment he went on Bill O'Reilly's show to clarify.

Trump loves giving people negative nicknames as personal attacks against them and he's gotten a lot of flack for it. Donald defends his way of attacking saying attacks on the intellectual level don't resonate well with the public because no one listens whereas the personal attacks do.

On August 28th Trump tweeted "A sad day for the Democrats. Kisten Gillibrand has dropped out of the Presidential Primary. I'm glad they never found out that she was the one I was really afraid of!"

Trump's rally in Orlando, Florida 2019 completely filled the 20,000 seat Amway Center.

For Trump's rally in El Paso, Texas 2019 roughly 30,000 people registered to attend.

Rather than spend his 100th day in office attending the White House Correspondents Dinner with its left-wing anti-Trump journalists and media figures, Trump went to Pennsylvania to hold a Trump Rally for his supporters. Trump became the first president since Reagan in 1981 to skip the dinner. That same day, a Morning Consult survey found that more American adults – 37% to 29% – trusted the White House over the media to tell the truth. In 2018 President Trump skipped the White House Correspondents' Dinner again, speaking at a campaign-style rally in Michigan instead. Trump then skipped the dinner for the third year in a row in 2019, holding another rally.

Trump raised $108 million in the second quarter of 2019 for his reelection.

Trump set a Presidential record raising $125 million in the third quarter of 2019 for his reelection, nearly double what Obama raised in 2011.

Trump and the Republican National convention set a new

historical record for money raised for a re-election bid at this point in a campaign. With a year still to go before the election, they have raised $300 million and $158 million of that is cash on hand.

Trump is selling plastic straws and sharpies, which are netting his campaign nearly one million dollars in cash for his re-election bid.

President Donald Trump received the enforcement of Indian Prime Minister Narendra Modi in September of 2019. They shared a stage in Houston, Texas and Modi said that India has a "true friend" in the White House. With more than 50,000 Indian Americans they're an influential voter base.

For the entire month of August 2019, the DNC raised 7.9 million dollars for their election campaign whereas Trump raised $15 million in California alone that month.

Bill O'Reilly has taken credit for suggesting Trump make his re-election campaign slogan "Keep America Great."

Trump broke the news on twitter that his rally at the SNHU Arena in Manchester, New Hampshire had broken Elton John's attendance record for the venue. Liberal media outlets called him a liar and shared images of empty seats but Manchester Deputy Fire Marshal Mitchell Cady confirmed that there were 11,500 people in attendance (200 more than Elton John) and an additional 8,000 people outside the venue who wanted to attend.

As an example of how the Republican Party became the "party of Trump," the RNC hired pro-Trump Kayleigh McEnany as its national spokeswoman. RNC Chairwoman Ronna Romney McDaniel also was pro-Trump. By 2018, the Republican Party was adopting

President Trump's positions on various issues such as trade and immigration. President Trump increased his influence over the GOP through the election of strongly pro-Trump individuals to the leadership of the various state parties.

November 2019. Of over sixteen thousand voters who attended a Trump rally in Mississippi were polled. The results showed that 27% were registered democrats, 24% said they had voted only once or less in the last four elections, and half the attendees said they had never voted for a President before. In addition 20% of people who attended were black.

Trump Quotes.
Facts 985-1001

"What separates the winners from the losers is how a person reacts to each new twist of fate."

"Money was never a big motivation for me, except as a way to keep score. The real excitement is playing the game."

"In real life, if I were firing you, I'd tell you what a great job you did, how fantastic you are, and how you can do better someplace else. If somebody steals, that's different, but generally speaking, you want to let them down as lightly as possible. It's not very pleasant thing. I don't like firing people."

"I'm the Ernest Hemingway of 140 characters."

"What truly matters is not which party controls our government, but whether our government is controlled by the people. January 20th 2017, will be remembered as the day the people became the rulers of this nation again. The forgotten men and women of our country will by forgotten no longer. Everyone is listening to you now."

"It's not like I'm anti-China. I just think it's ridiculous that we allow them to do what they're doing to this country, with the manipulation of the currency, that you write about and understand, and all of the other things that they do."

"I grew up in New York City, a town with different races, religions, and peoples. It breeds tolerance."

"I think Ronald Reagan was one of the great presidents, period, not just recently. I thought he had the demeanor. I thought he had the bearing. I thought he had the thought process."

"A little more moderation would be good. Of course, my life hasn't exactly been one of moderation."

"If you love what you do, if you love going to the office, if you really like it - not just say it, but really like it - it keeps you young and energized. I really love what I do."

"If you're interested in 'balancing' work and pleasure, stop trying to balance them. Instead, make your work more pleasurable."

"I think I will be a great president having to do with the military and also having to do with taking care of our vets."

"The pact we have with Japan is interesting. Because if somebody attacks us, Japan does not have to help. If somebody attacks Japan, we have to help Japan."

"I describe Jeb Bush as a 'low-energy' individual, and unfortunately for him, that stuck. And it's true: he's a low-energy person. That doesn't make him a bad person."

"You have to think anyway, so why not think big."

In 2019 when a French reporter asked Trump why he thought the U.S. has such a low unemployment rate compared to France, Trump responded, "Well… maybe we have a better President than you do."

"In the end, you're measured not by how much you undertake but by what you finally accomplish."

Made in the USA
Middletown, DE
22 November 2020

24756579R00106